Potatoes

Bodo A. Schieren

Potatoes

THUNDER BAY
P·R·E·S·S

Thunder Bay Press
5880 Oberlin Drive
Suite 400
San Diego, CA 92121

First published in the United States by Thunder Bay Press, 1994
Published in Germany in 1989 by Südwest Verlag GmbH & Co. KG, Munich
German language edition and photographs © Südwest Verlag GmbH & Co. KG, 1989
American language edition © 1994 Transedition Books, a division of Andromeda Oxford Limited,
11-15 The Vineyard, Abingdon, Oxon OX14 3PX, England

Photography: Bodo A. Schieren
Recipes and food arrangement: Jürgen Suré
Translation: Isabel Varea in association with First Edition Translations Ltd, Cambridge

Schieren, Bodo A.
    Potatoes / Bodo A. Schieren
        p.   cm.
    Includes index
    ISBN 1-57145-004-1 : $15.95
        1. Cookery (Potatoes)   2. Potatoes.   I. Title.
TX803.P8S35   1994
641.6'521--dc20   94-14125

Printed in 1994 in Spain

ISBN 1 - 57145 - 004 - 1

Contents

Foreword

*T*he potato, which is native to South America, has, along with bread, become one of our staple foods. Many of us cherish childhood memories of the joys of munching french fries and potato chips or tucking into mashed or baked potatoes. As adults, we appreciate not only the tasty snacks potatoes offer, but also the nutritional value they provide to our diet.

To the cook, the potato offers a challenge, calling for imagination and ingenuity. The humble spud is not there simply to soak up the gravy. It can be prepared in all kinds of simple and sophisticated ways, to be served hot or cold, as an accompaniment or main course, with only the simplest seasonings or with such gourmet ingredients as salmon or caviar.

Potatoes *begins with the history of the potato, and describes how it is grown and harvested. It provides information about calorie content and nutritional values, about herbs and spices, and about what to look for when buying potatoes and how to store them. Above all, the clearly explained recipes are designed to encourage you to experience for yourself just how refined and versatile potatoes can be. The book's elegant presentation and fascinating and informative text promise not only a feast for the eyes, but also culinary delights of the highest order.*

Potato

Danish Kartoffel

Dutch aardappel

Finnish peruna

French pomme de terre

German Kartoffel

Greek *γεω,υηλον*

Hungarian burgonys, pityóka, kolompír, krumpli

Italian patata

Latin Solanum tuberosum

Norwegian Potet, Potetes

Portuguese batata

Spanish patata

Swedish jordpäron, potates

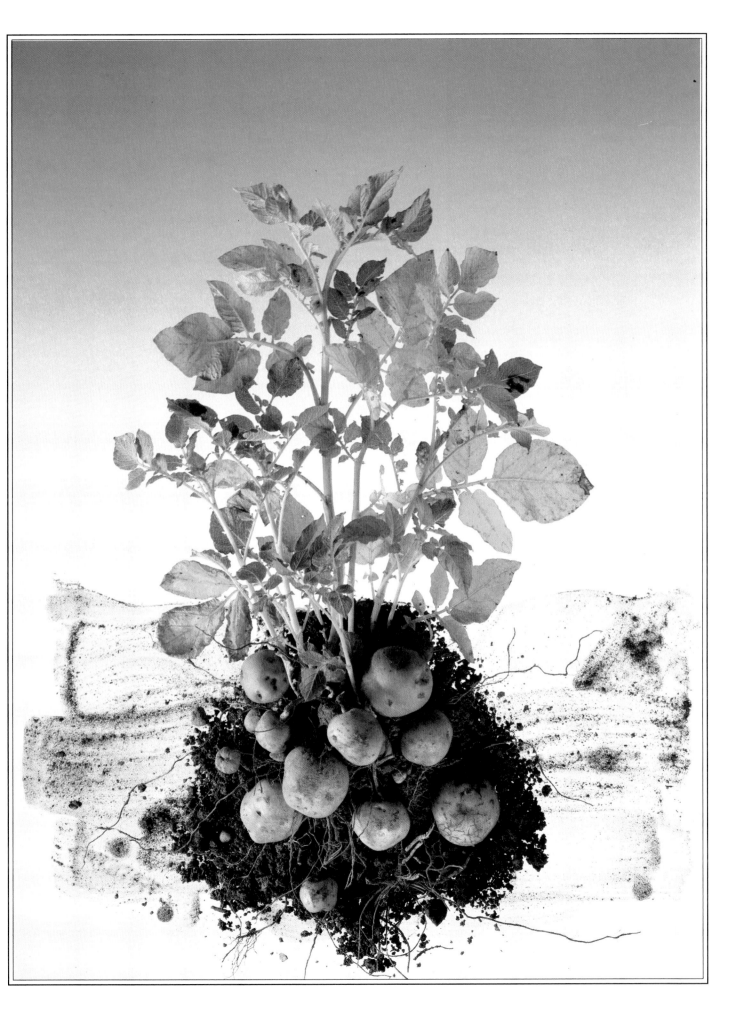

Drawings by Poma de Ayala, from the book Los Mezes i Años, *1584–1614*

Introducing the Potato

The potato is an unassuming vegetable. Unlike many others, it does not catch the eye with its bright color or strong flavor. You can buy it anywhere, and it is easy to cook. Indeed, it is one of the mainstays of our diet. However, this tuber is a homely deity, to whom human understanding has assigned a variety of roles during its long life. The potato has been seen as a god of nature and the work of the devil, a miracle cure and the height of depravity, a means of survival and an aphrodisiac. For years, potatoes were thought to be fattening, and many people refused to eat them. Today, however, they have finally taken on a new, glittering image as a healthy, low-calorie and palatable source of energy.

The tempestuous career of the potato began in the heights of the Andes, in Peru, Bolivia, Ecuador and Chile. According to evidence found among 8,000-year-old Peruvian burial objects, potatoes have been cultivated in this part of the world since the dawn of time. Maize and potatoes were the staple diet of the earliest inhabitants of the Andean region. Potatoes, however, can be cultivated at up to 10,000 feet above sea-level, where maize will no longer grow. Well before the time of the Incas, the ancient Quechua Indians not only consumed potatoes, they also worshipped them. To them, Nature was a divine force and the potato was a life-giving goddess who had to be appeased to keep her in a benevolent mood. We know that the Incas also revered the potato because they made potato-shaped jugs and other cult objects to place in the tombs of the dead.

Before the Europeans set out to colonize America and the rest of the world, the vast Inca nation was considered invincible by surrounding peoples. The Incas were experts in making provision for times of famine. It was they who invented freeze-dried potatoes. The Incas would leave the potatoes out in the open to freeze in the chill night air. They were then thawed in the daytime under the blazing sun, and left until they dried out, all the water content having been extracted in a completely natural way. After that, they would keep indefinitely. These edible "stones" could be soaked at any time to make them soft again, and then they could be eaten.

When they discovered the Americas, the Spanish conquistadors were more than a little surprised by these stone-hard tubers. They were first reported by Pedro de Cieza de León, a member of a Spanish expedition to the high Andes in 1538:

It is very cold there, no maize grows, neither are there any trees. Papas are the mainstay of the inhabitants. They dry them in the sun and store them from one harvest to the next. They are then

10

From left to right: Sowing seed potatoes, Weeding the field, Harvest, Filling the potato store

called chuño. *When boiled, they become as tender as chestnuts. Their skin is no thicker than a truffle's.*

Supposedly in the same year, de León's comrade-in-arms, Juan de Castellanos, noted that in the village of Sorocata in the River Magdalena region (now Colombia) there were "maize, beans and truffles". He found that the so-called "truffles" were very good to eat. He wrote: "They have floury roots, and a good flavor. They are a valuable asset to the Indians and a delicious food, even for Spaniards."

It was not long before the conquistadors were bringing potatoes back to Spain as souvenirs. One of the first recorded offerings of potatoes was presented by a loyal subject to King Philip II in 1565. The gift package may well have included a list of the healing properties attributed to potatoes by the Indians: they laid raw potato on broken bones, rubbed the forehead with raw potato to relieve headaches, carried a potato in the pocket to ward off rheumatism, and ate potatoes to cure indigestion. In any case, Philip sent the newly discovered vegetable to Pope Pius V, in the hope of improving the state of papal health. The benevolent pontiff gave a few tubers to an ailing cardinal in the Netherlands, who then shared his present with the Prefect of Mons. The latter seems to have planted his potatoes in his garden in order to pass some samples on to the then-famous botanist Charles d'Ecluse, who, following the current fashion for Latinized names, called himself Carolus Clusius. In 1573 Clusius became gardens superintendent to the Holy Roman Emperor Rudolph II and was also responsible for the various pleasure parks of Count Wilhelm IV of Hesse. To please his illustrious employers, Clusius embellished their borders with the rare potato plants, with their sweetly perfumed pink, blue and mauve blossoms.

Proudly, the Emperor and Count sent cuttings to their friends and relations. Count Wilhelm wrote to Christian I, Prince-Elector of Saxony:

We are sending Your Highness a plant, which we obtained from Italy a few years ago and which is called taratouphli. *This plant grows in the ground and has pretty flowers, a pleasant odor and, underneath, roots from which many* tubera *hang; these, when boiled, are good to eat. They must first be boiled in water, until the outer skin comes off, then the water must be poured away and the potato finally seethed in butter until done.*

So people knew that the potato was edible. None the less, in Europe around the turn of the seventeenth century it was grown chiefly as an exotic ornamental or medicinal plant in the parks of spiritual and temporal rulers. It also flourished in the herb gardens of medical schools and universities, and probably in the kitchen gardens of monastic communities or wealthy aristocratic families. In botanical catalogues the potato appeared under garden and healing plants.

It was highly prized by doctors, botanists and princes, not least because they believed it to have certain mysterious powers, discreetly claiming that it "enhances the conjugal function". Potato recipes were tried out in the kitchens of many noble houses, but with not much success. With its delicate, bland taste, it could not compete with the flavors of the many spices and other delicacies that were by this time emerging from every corner of the world. Only later would large-scale potato cultivation begin in Europe.

It started in Spain. Accounts kept at the hospital in Seville reveal that from 1573 onwards locally grown potatoes were regularly delivered to the kitchens. The crews of the many ships heading for the South American colonies had long been accustomed to feeding on potatoes. The Spaniards had quickly learned to provision their ships with the Incas" crops. On ships where potatoes were on the menu, a fortunate side-effect was that the crews escaped the ravages of scurvy, a disease dreaded by every seafarer.

Potatoes also found their way to the British Isles. English history books have long credited the much-admired Sir Francis Drake, famed for his circumnavigation of the globe, with the introduction of potatoes to Britain. Historians always refer to a banquet on April 4, 1581 at which Drake served Queen Elizabeth I with potatoes brought back from his around-the-world voyage. However, the menu card, which still survives, shows that the feast included *batatas*, which was the name given to sweet potatoes in the West Indies at that time.

The "real" potatoes were, in fact, in the luggage of Thomas Heriot, a British geographer. After a journey of exploration to the colony of Virginia, Heriot returned home in 1586 on one of Drake's ships. Drake had captured some Spanish galleons in the Caribbean. In order to inspect the spoils and reload, he remained in dock at Cartagena for six weeks. It is most likely that Heriot met some of the local potato suppliers when they came aboard. The fact that Heriot was already carrying an assortment of plants from Virginia gave rise to the erroneous belief that the potato came from the same area, and that it was Drake who had discovered it. It appears in the great English book by John Gerard, *Herball or General History of Plants* as "Potato of Virginia". Since people like to believe in big names and enjoy good stories, Drake was accorded many literary tributes as the reputed discoverer of the potato.

However, although Drake did not discover it, he did indeed contribute to the spread of the potato. When his superior, Sir Walter Ralegh, retired to his estates in Ireland, Drake is said to have sent him a sack of seed potatoes. This sack may well have laid the foundation for the staple crop that was to feed the Irish people. Those not convinced by this story may prefer the following version: following the defeat of the Spanish Armada in 1588, many ships were wrecked off the coast of Ireland. Irish peasants who plundered the wrecks would have found potatoes on board and brought them ashore.

However it became established there, the potatos use as a food in Ireland helped to introduce it to Germany in this capacity. Although they were already thriving in the gardens of the German nobility, potatoes were not eaten by the ordinary people of Germany until the "Glorious Revolution" of 1668, when German mercenaries fought in Ireland against the Stuart King James II, and were sustained mainly by Irish potatoes. Other mercenaries engaged in the War of the Spanish Succession tried growing potatoes in the Netherlands. Refugees fleeing to Germany from religious persecution in Spain and the Netherlands may have brought potatoes with them. German monasteries began to use potatoes to feed the poor. There is evidence that they were cultivated throughout Germany by the end of the seventeenth century.

Admittedly, the potato did not gain immediate universal acceptance in Europe. Further expansion was hindered by prejudice and superstition. The peasants had their own way of putting potatoes to the test: they threw them to their dogs. When the animals refused to eat them, it was assumed that they were not fit for human consumption. As the potato belongs to the same family as deadly nightshade, it was credited with diabolic powers. Some people said that potatoes contained narcotic substances, others claimed that they were poisonous, while still others believed that they caused such diseases as gout, anemia, skin rashes and rheumatism. Whatever information

scholars may have had about this fruit of the earth simply did not get through to the rest of the population, particularly the rumor that frequent consumption of potatoes increased sexual urges to an extraordinary degree – a fact unlikely to safeguard the morals of the poor. It was only when the cereal crops failed in Germany between 1743 and 1755 that large numbers of farmers there were converted to the cause of potatoes. Frederick the Great commanded his subjects in the Eastern Provinces and Silesia to grow them, threatening any who refused with severe penalties. He needed well-fed, contented underlings, as well as strong, battle-ready soldiers for such conflicts as the Seven Years" War, in which the Prussian Army fought against the troops of Saxony, Austria, Russia, Sweden and France.

Right at the beginning of the war a Frenchman was taken prisoner by the Prussians. During his captivity the military apothecary Antoine Auguste Parmentier, then twenty years old, became acquainted with potatoes and later made them popular in his homeland. Until that time, the French had regarded the potato as a decorative motif. Whole dinner services painted with potato designs were ordered from porcelain manufacturers for pre-Revolutionary Versailles. Marie Antoinette's evening gowns were embroidered with potato flowers, and she used real blossoms to adorn her elaborate hairstyles. Meanwhile, Parmentier set out to promote the potato as an alternative to bread, which was becoming ever more expensive. He

was the winner of a competition, organized by the Academy of Science, to find ways to relieve hunger. However, he used trickery to encourage farmers to cultivate potatoes. In 1785 he convinced Louis XVI to allow him to plant a field of potatoes in the countryside near Paris. He then placed the field under military guard – but only in daylight hours. This made the peasants curious. These must be very valuable plants, they thought, and promptly stole them under cover of night.

Parmentier was a gourmet who created many potato recipes, the most famous of which are Potage Parmentier, an exquisite, thick potato soup, and Pommes Parmentier, diced potatoes fried with chives. Since Parmentier's day, the French have constantly invented sophisticated potato dishes. As a result, in France the potato never acquired the reputation it had elsewhere in Europe, as food for the poor. None the less, it gradually became accepted throughout Europe as an important part of subsistence diets, and by the beginning of the nineteenth century potatoes had become everyday fare for ordinary people.

There was a sudden outpouring of treatises on the potato, its cultivation and storage, its different varieties, as well as recipes for potato flour, dumplings, puddings and cakes, and instructions for the use of the vegetable in the production of glue, soap, beer and wine. There were even suggestions for recycling the leaves and skins for manufacturing paper.

Particularly well-received were ideas for distilling potato spirit. This was a way of immediately preserving the highly perishable potato into a durable and easily saleable form.

There were two important effects of the increasingly widespread cultivation of the potato: a steep rise in population and a decline in the cultivation of other field crops. This ultimately had disastrous results. Repeated failures of the potato crop in the early 1840s led to famine in many parts of Europe. Ireland was the most notable example. After the potato began to be cultivated there late in the seventeenth century the population rose from about 5 million in 1800 to about 8 million in 1845, and the majority of these people were poor and lived on a diet mainly of potatoes. Potato production was not only intensive, but limited to one variety. When the fungal disease called blight infected one crop, it spread across the country like wildfire, resulting in the "potato famines" of 1845, 1846 and 1848. Hundreds of thousands of people died. Of those who survived, hundreds of thousands more emigrated, most of them to North America.

Many people believe that this is when the potato arrived in the United States, particularly as it is often called the "Irish potato". In fact, some scholars believe that the potato was introduced to the American colonies as early as 1622, when it is reputed to have been brought from Bermuda by Virginia colonists. It is known for certain that potato cultivation was undertaken in New Hampshire in 1719 by immigrants who brought plants with them from Ireland, and this is probably when it got its "Irish" label, in order to distinguish it from the native sweet potato.

In the nineteenth century industrialization meant that fewer laborers were needed on the land, so workers flocked to the large towns and cities to find work. With the spread of the railroads, potatoes, as well as other foods, could be quickly transported to the centers of population. People everywhere were eating potatoes and becoming more creative in their preparation. It was in 1853 in Saratoga Springs, New York that George Crum, a native American, created the first potato chips. Although destined to become one of the most popular potato products in the world, potato chips did not become widely known in the United States until after the Civil War, and the first factory dedicated to their exclusive manufacture was not built until 1925.

In each of the two world wars potatoes assumed a special importance, particularly in Europe. During the Second World War, for example, imports to Britain were severely restricted,and supplies of fresh produce, particularly vegetables, were limited. Because the potato plant is so prolific, millions of extra tons could be, and were, grown to keep the people fed in face of the other shortages. People relied heavily on the potato, and found a variety of imaginative ways in which to prepare them. When better times came and there was plenty of food for everybody, potatoes retained their popularity, particularly in the form of potato chips and french fries.

However, the obsession with slimming that began to sweep the world in the 1970s posed a threat to the traditional place of potatoes in diets everywhere: they were – and, by some people, still are – believed to be fattening. Fortunately for the sensational spud, as the trend towards healthy eating boomed in the 1980s the true worth of the potato was recognized: it contains far more vitamins and minerals and far fewer calories than was previously thought, and is a good source of dietary fiber.

If potato consumption had declined, it now enjoyed a renaissance. Top restaurant chefs and cookery writers led the way, creating ever more refined potato side-dishes, and even introducing potato-based main courses. Manufacturers, who had already produced canned, powdered and frozen raw potatoes and potato products for the convenience of consumers, now introduced oven-ready and microwave french fries so that this favorite food could be eaten even by people on low-fat diets. There is also, of course, a selection of different varieties of fresh potatoes available in food stores and supermarkets throughout the year. This book is dedicated to all those who join us in celebrating that most versatile of all vegetables, the potato.

How Potatoes Are Grown

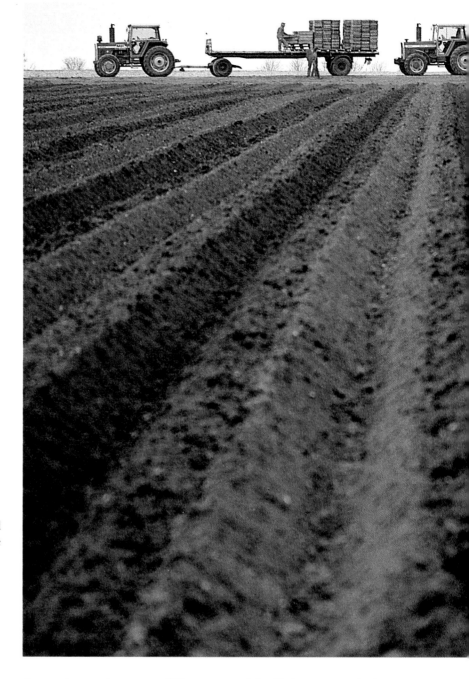

Potatoes grow practically anywhere in the world – from Greenland to Egypt, from the Arctic Circle to the tropics – but nurturing them is no easy task. Firstly, the soil has to be well prepared by plowing every fall, and removing stones and clods from the soil in spring, which helps to reduce bruising or damage to the potatoes when they are being harvested. The field is then fertilized. The seed potatoes must be planted on level ground in furrows and then earthed up. They need a fair, but not excessive, amount of moisture, and watering when in bloom. The rows must also be kept free of weeds. At one time many farmers were slaves to the hoe. Whole families, including children, would share the back-breaking work of growing potatoes. Today technical expertise is more essential to farmers than physical fitness, as they employ modern machinery to manage their crop. For example, a potato planter, equipped with a series of cups on an endless belt or chain, with a self-compensating device that adds a potato if an empty cup is

detected, can plant up to 600 tubers under the soil every minute. The process is often supervised manually to ensure the seeds are evenly spaced, so that the crop will be a uniform size. Some farmers grow new potatoes under plastic tunnels to protect them from late frosts, and all potato growers have to guard their crops against diseases.

According to variety, each single seed potato produces up to twenty-five new tubers. Potato cultivation has become a science in its own

right. If the same varieties are sown year after year their quality deteriorates, so potatoes are constantly crossbred or replaced. Specialists in plant propagation are continually creating new varieties of seed potatoes. New types of potato are designed to have not only a pleasing flavor, but also firm skins, an even size and resistance to disease. Some have to meet the needs of particular markets: the goal for many growers is to produce a larger yield in the shortest possible time, while development experts are on the

16

lookout for varieties suited to climatic conditions in countries of the Third World, and the food industry wants tubers with a high starch content, which are good for drying or freezing and easy to process.

It takes ten to twelve years before a new variety is ready for the market. To achieve the desired characteristics, two types of potato plant are cross-pollinated. If pollination is successful, a new plant will grow. The seeds from its green berries are scattered in a special seed bed to produce sturdy seedlings. Of the number produced, only a tiny percentage eventually become a new variety. For example, if propagation specialists produced about a million potato seedlings, after a year about 40,000 would survive, and after six or seven years of further selection 40 new varieties would emerge. These would undergo around three years of further testing – including a number of tastings – by experts. After passing these tests, between eight and ten new varieties would appear on the market. The number remains constant nationally, for as new types emerge, varieties whose quality has diminished or are well past their best are withdrawn.

Misshapen and grossly oversized specimens do not stand a chance in this selection process. Only occasionally do we see photographs of amateur growers proudly displaying giant tubers. In recent times genetic research has concentrated more strongly on the potato. Scientists are attempting to create potatoes "from within", or, to be more exact, from the DNA at the heart of the plant cell.

The isolation and transfer of genes have produced tubers that are no longer prone to certain blights, which used to be treated by chemical means. Researchers are now working on the creation of the "super-spud". They are reported to be increasing the protein content of potatoes through genetic engineering.

From Grower to Consumer

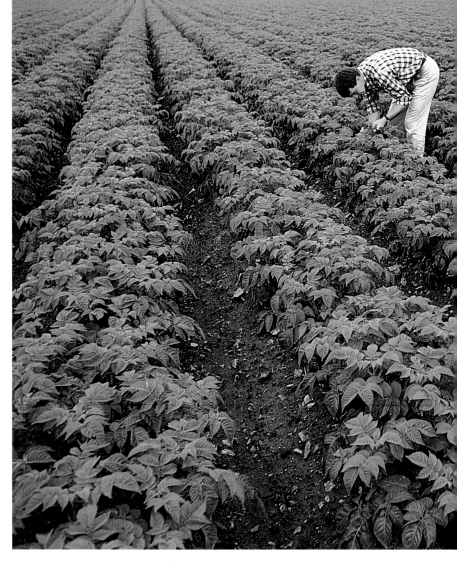

Consumers want nicely shaped tubers of similar size, not necessarily very large, but with healthy, smooth, unblemished skins. To produce this result the grower has to plant the right kind of potatoes on his land. At one time potato fields were a blaze of different colored blossoms because a mixture of seeds had been sown. Now farmers would be alarmed if their potato blossoms were the "wrong" shade. They avoid this situation by buying fresh plants every year. Then the plants are sprouted and protected against pests and disease: nothing that can be avoided is left to chance. Even so, it is often Mother Nature herself who does the most damage. Unseasonal night frosts and rainy summers can adversely affect the quality of the crop. Tubers from the same field can vary in consistency, flavor and storage qualities from one year to the next.

Modern farmers have the harvest well organized. A single machine can do almost everything: a complete potato harvester picks the potatoes, separates them from clods of soil and lifts them on to a belt, where they are sorted. Only those who have harvested potatoes by hand will fully appreciate the benefits of such technology! Human sorters remove any remaining stones and clumps of earth, and reject any misshapen, shriveled, bruised or damaged specimens as the tubers roll along

conveyor belts to depots, where the freshly harvested potatoes are packed and immediately transported to their various markets.

These highly mechanized harvesting techniques can be only good news for potato-lovers. Very few potatoes are damaged during lifting, and modern distribution methods mean that these light-sensitive tubers lose barely any of their nutrients. The food industry also makes good use of these advantages. Since the "raw material" is delivered fresh from the fields, it can be stored or carefully processed while retaining most of its goodness. We cannot expect quite so much of potatoes stored at home, even as far as flavor is concerned, because the conditions there are not as precisely controlled and, unless we are lucky enough to buy them from a farm shop, the potatoes have spent time in the distribution chain before they reach our local stores and supermarkets.

In fact, although the percentage varies, in most industrialized countries a large proportion of the annual potato crop is processed. For example, in Australia, which grows 1.2 million ton of potatoes annually, about 49 per cent is used for processing; Britain, which produces about 7.5 million tons a year, sends about 37 per cent directly to food manufacturers; while the United States, which harvests about 20 million tons in a year, delivers about 56 per cent to the food-processing industry. In

whatever form we eat them, potatoes are still one of our favorite foods. It is interesting to note that Ireland, which has been a potato-loving nation since the seventeenth century, still leads the world in per-capita consumption, at 309 pounds a year. Elsewhere the potato competes with rice and pasta as a major carbohydrate and a "fast food", but annual per-capita consumption in Britain is still about 220 pounds, in Australia about 140 pounds and in United States about 130 pounds.

Potatoes Are So Healthy

Every potato is a power pack, brimming with goodness. In theory, we could eat only potatoes, supplemented with the occasional glass of milk or the odd egg (to provide animal protein), and the body would suffer no dietary deficiency. As we are in the happy position of enjoying a far more mixed diet, we do not eat enough potatoes. This is a pity, say health practitioners, listing all the good things to be found in potatoes.

Potatoes are full of vitamins

Potatoes contain Vitamins C, B1 (thiamine), B2 (riboflavin), B3, and B6 (pyridoxine). The most important of these is Vitamin C. The entire recommended daily amount for an adult can be found in 14 ounces of potatoes. The vitamin content is at its peak at harvest time, and decreases during storage. More vitamins disappear during cooking. Potatoes boiled in their skins and large baked potatoes lose about 20–40 per cent of their Vitamin C alone, while french fries and roast potatoes lose about 30–40 per cent, and peeled, boiled potatoes lose as much as 30–50 per cent.

Potatoes contain high-grade protein

The quality of protein we consume matters more than the quantity. Potato protein is an ideal blend of essential amino acids. Since the body functions most efficiently on a mixture of vegetable and animal proteins, from a health point of view the best combination is potato protein with milk or egg, such as creamy mashed potatoes with a fried egg or fried potatoes with scrambled egg.

Potatoes are rich in minerals

The potato's high potassium content means it is an ideal way to offset the surplus acid in such foods as meat and certain kinds of vegetables. Many people (women more than men) suffer from iron and magnesium deficiencies, particularly those who take part in a lot of sport. Those who eat potatoes on a regular basis have no need to take iron or magnesium supplements.

Potatoes are low in calories

Many people would be surprised to learn that 3 ½ ounces of boiled potatoes contain only 75–80 calories. Even french fries, which contain 230 calories per 3 ½ ounces because of the fat in which they are cooked, have less than half the number of calories in a piece of chocolate cake of the same weight. If you ate nothing but potatoes, you would have to consume almost 6 ½ pounds of boiled potatoes or 2 ⅕ pounds of french fries a day in order to meet a daily requirement of 2,200 calories!

Potatoes contain complex carbohydrates

It used to be unjustly claimed that carbohydrates led to excess weight. We now know that they are the body's most important source of energy. Among the complex carbohydrates are starch and fiber. During the digestive process cooked potato starch is converted into carbohydrate and stored as an energy reserve in the liver and muscles. Fiber is a vital aid to digestion. It absorbs a great deal of body fluid and expands enormously. This increased bulk encourages more efficient bowel function. Fiber-rich foods stay in the system only half as long as those with little fiber. Most importantly, fiber enables the body to expel far more quickly harmful substances absorbed from the environment, as well as the body's own toxins and waste products.

Potatoes are very low in fat

The fat content of potatoes is only 0.01–0.1 per cent. This tiny quantity includes "good" essential fatty acids.

Potato Diets and Remedies

Some doctors and health practitioners recommend a potato-rich diet to people with various illnesses.

The potato diet

We are warned against many diets, not because they allow too little food, but because the choice of what to eat is so limited. No danger of this with the potato diet! Although you are eating less than usual, potatoes are so nutritious that the body gets all the nourishment it needs. You will not go hungry either: since potatoes are so low in calories, on a daily allowance of 1,000 calories you can eat your fill. If you divide 1 ¼ pounds of potatoes between your midday and evening meals, you will still have just about 500 calories to spare for a variety of other food, and for breakfast. The potato diet has another virtue: the high potassium content helps the body flush away excess fluid.

Diabetes

Many diabetics are overweight. Their bodies must have a steady supply of carbohydrates, but not in excessive quantities, to avoid creating too much sugar in the blood. On a potato diet, diabetics can lose weight without any harmful side-effects.

Kidney deficiency

To avoid having to resort to dialysis, people whose kidneys fail to excrete waste products must eat little protein, which must be of high quality. Because of its biological efficiency, the potato and egg diet is especially good for kidney patients.

Gout

Gout, the so called "rich man's complaint", is caused mainly by consuming too much meat and animal fat. One of the symptoms is the overproduction of uric acid. The most important part of treatment is a diet low in this acid. Potatoes contain very little uric acid and therefore can be the main ingredient in an anti-gout diet.

High blood pressure

When certain bodily functions are disturbed, the kidneys excrete insufficient sodium, which leads to raised blood pressure (hypertension). Sufferers are prescribed an extremely low-sodium diet. This means eating foods naturally low in sodium and avoiding or restricting the use of salt in their preparation. Potatoes are the perfect low-sodium food, so patients with high blood pressure are urged to include frequent "potato days" in their diet.

Celiac disease

So far no cure has been found for this intolerance of any type of grain. Sufferers find potatoes easy to take, and can make them the mainstay of their diet.

Potatoes as a home remedy

Not everyone wants to carry a potato in their pocket or hang one around their neck to ward off rheumatism – even though the Incas are reported to have found it helpful. Here are a few proven, easy-to-follow home remedies.

For diarrhea, eat unsalted potatoes mashed with water.

For heartburn and flatulence, drink freshly squeezed juice of raw potatoes first thing in the morning (some practitioners of alternative medicine even prescribe this treatment for stomach ulcers).

For stomach pain and sore throat, make a compress by placing hot, unpeeled, boiled potatoes in a linen bag, or wrap them in a dish towel. Crush them coarsely, then apply to the affected part.

Buying and Storing Potatoes

Potatoes are carefully cleaned, sorted and graded before they reach the stores and supermarkets to ensure that you find only healthy, firm potatoes with smooth skins. The slight green patches on potato skins sometimes seen in supermarkets are caused by exposure to light and sometimes by the temperature at which they are stored or displayed. This kind of greening is usually superficial and easily removed by peeling. (Darker greening, which happens when potatoes are exposed to light while they are growing, is unhealthy, and affected potatoes are normally discarded during sorting.) Potatoes are also sensitive to damp, so you should not accept those displayed outdoors if they have been exposed to rain.

The plastic bags in which potatoes are often sold are not a brilliant idea. As the temperature fluctuates, the potatoes sweat, and can become moldy. If this is the most convenient way for you to buy them, transfer them to an open basket or a paper bag as soon as you get them home.

Buy potatoes in quantities that you plan to use within a short period of time. Store them in a cool, dark place with good air circulation, not in the refrigerator.

If you are planning to peel the potatoes before cooking, do so only when your are ready to use them: peeled potatoes that are kept sitting in water lose more of their nutrients than those that are peeled and cooked immediately.

Utensils

The following pages show very useful kitchen tools designed for tackling potatoes.

Potato peelers

Paring knife

Vegetable knife

Cook's knife

Serrated knife

Potato fork

Radish cutter for
making potato spirals

Vegetable corer

Potato baller

25

Fine grater

Hash-brown grater

Boiled potato slicer

Boiled potato grater

Wooden potato masher

Wire basket for baking potatoes on an open fire or barbecue

Metal potato masher

Potato press

Cooking is much more fun — and takes less time — if you have the right equipment to hand. Apart from their usefulness, simple, shiny utensils displayed on a rack are an esthetic delight for many cooks, and quite the nicest way to decorate a kitchen wall. The choice of tools depends on individual need and personal taste. If you never prepare potato purée, a masher is, of course, unnecessary. On the other hand, if you like to experiment, the right utensils will broaden your scope. Take the examples on page 25: we have used a vegetable corer and a radish cutter on raw potatoes. The result is amusing potato spirals, which, when deep-fried, make an interesting change from straight-cut french fries.

Slotted ladle

Ladle for deep-fried foods

French fries basket

Whisk

Double basket for potato nests

All You Need for Deep-Frying

Deep fryer

If you are a lover of fried foods, it is worth investing in a deep-fryer. This keeps the fat at the constant high temperature needed for frying. The hotter the fat, the quicker the food will cook, and the less fat it will absorb, which means it will contain fewer calories.

French fries cutter

SAFRAN

Glossary

The potato's own mild flavor blends perfectly with a wide range of spices and strong-tasting herbs. It is best not to use too great a mixture, however. Add generous quantities, but only one herb or spice at a time, so that its flavor really penetrates.

Allspice
This pungent spice is made from unripe allspice berries. Not only is the flavor peppery, it also has hints of cloves, nutmeg and cinnamon. Allspice is used in the same way as these three spices.

Bay leaves
Fresh leaves of the evergreen bay tree or bush are more aromatic than when dried, the form in which they are most often used. If you particularly enjoy their strong, slightly bitter taste, you could grow a tree in a large pot or in a garden. Bay leaves tend to be used too sparingly; instead of half a leaf, you can quite happily add two or three to soups or stews.

Capers
These flowerbuds of a Mediterranean bush are made edible by pickling in brine or vinegar. The smaller they are, the more subtle their flavor. Their sharp, bitter flavor makes them ideal for substantial potato salads, and they also add a distinctive tang to mixed salads.

Caraway
The seed of a plant with finely divided leaves and small, whitish flowers, caraway is used to flavor hearty dishes. The taste is pleasant but strong, so caraway seeds should be used sparingly, with one exception: you can add a healthy dose to the water when boiling potatoes in their skins, so that the flavor can penetrate the skins.

Cardamom
This plant, which is a relative of ginger, is grown mainly in southeast Asia, and its dried seed pods are used in cooking. To retain their sweetish, resinous taste, buy whole pods and crush them in a pestle and mortar when you need them. Exotic cardamom may seem an unusual ingredient to combine with potatoes, but why not give it a try?

Cayenne pepper
Made from ground red chili peppers, cayenne is hot and aromatic. Buy it only in small quantities and use it quickly, as it soon loses its flavor but retains its nip. Use cayenne in hot and spicy dishes such as potato bread.

Chervil
A delicate herb that can be grown in a pot, and is most aromatic in spring and fall. Fresh chervil leaves have a slightly sweet, aniseed flavor. Chervil adds a distinctive note to potato soup, and is good in springtime with new potatoes.

Chili peppers
Fresh chili peppers are spicy; dried ones are simply hot. The rule is the smaller the peppers, the more fiery they are. Finely chopped or crushed with a pestle and mortar, they add extra zest to fried potatoes. Preserved chilies — often labeled *pepperoni* — are best used straight out of the jar; they are not very good for cooking. In the pickling process they take on a slightly sour flavor as well as their characteristic fieriness.

Chives
Easy to grow in a pot or garden, chives have an onion flavor and can be used in all savory dishes. To bring out their fresh tang, snip them with kitchen shears and sprinkle over food just before serving; they should not be cooked. For a change, you can arrange a bunch of fine stems on top of the finished dish. Chive flowers also make an attractive decoration.

Cinnamon
This commonly used spice is the bark of a type of bay tree growing in Asia, which rolls up as it is peeled from the tree. The thinner the bark is shaved, the more delicate the cinnamon flavor. The finest and sweetest cinnamon comes from Sri Lanka and is sold in sticks. Other varieties of cinnamon, usually rather more bitter and spicy, are usually ground. As well as using cinnamon for cakes and desserts, small quantities can be added to sweet-and-sour dishes.

Cloves
Looking like tiny nails, cloves are the flowerbuds of a huge tropical tree. They must be picked before the flowers open. Because of their strong perfume and slightly woody flavor, they should be used sparingly.

Dillweed
This herb, with its feathery leaves, is available dried, but is even tastier fresh. Dill best retains its characteristic flavor when raw, or cooked only briefly. It is good with potato salad, or simply sprinkled over boiled potatoes. In Sweden smoked salmon is often served accompanied by potatoes in a béchamel and dill sauce.

Garlic
If you like garlic, you can add it to anything — except desserts. The problem for most people is the lingering odor. Nobody has yet found a really effective remedy, although chewing fresh parsley after eating garlic is said to help. It is also important to know that the younger and fresher the garlic, the more subtle the flavor and the less persistent the smell. True garlic lovers can add generous amounts, sliced or crushed in a garlic press, to fried potatoes, casseroles, and

potato salads. If you prefer only a hint of garlic, rub the salad bowl or skillet with a cut clove.

Juniper berries

The berries are gathered from wild juniper bushes (related to the cypress tree). The smaller the berries, the better the sharp, bitter-sweet flavor. They add interest to marinades and sauces. Juniper berries should be crushed before use. Do not use more than about three berries per person, otherwise the taste is overpowering.

Marjoram

It is marjoram that gives blood pudding and liver sausage their characteristic taste. Since dried marjoram has such a good flavor, it is seldom used fresh, although it is so much more delicious. Good in potato soup, marjoram also adds interest to fried and roast potatoes.

Mustard seeds

The white and black seeds have no smell. They acquire their characteristic hot mustardy taste only when soaked in water. Whole mustard seeds can be used to season dressings for potato salads and similar dishes.

Nutmeg

The term "nut" is misleading. Botanically speaking, nutmeg is the seed of the nutmeg tree, which grows to a height of up to 52 feet. The dried kernel is grated before use. Mace is the name given to the outer covering of the nutmeg. It has the same fragrance and the same spicy flavor as nutmeg, but is more intense. Nutmeg is sold whole or ground. It is a must for mashed potatoes, and is also delicious in potato gratins and gnocchi.

Oregano

Marjoram's wild relative, oregano grows around the Mediterranean and is sold dried. Oregano can be

used in the same dishes as marjoram.

Paprika

Dried peppers are ground to produce paprika. The more seeds and ribs that are used with the dried flesh, the hotter the flavor and the brighter the color. The label of some brands indicates mild, sweet or hot. Sweet paprika is aromatic with very little fieriness. Hot paprika has a pungent taste. The milder types of paprika turn bitter when fried, so it is best to use them in stews such as potato goulash.

Parsley

This is probably the most universal and most commonly used culinary herb. Flat-leaved parsley has a stronger flavor than the curly variety, and both are easy to grow in the garden or in a flowerpot on the windowsill. One of its classic uses is in parsley potatoes.

Pepper

There are three different types of pepper. Black pepper berries are picked while still unripe, then dried. They have a hot and fiery taste. White pepper is made from ripe, peeled berries of the pepper plant, and has a milder flavor. Green pepper berries are also picked before they are ripe, and can be used fresh, pickled or freeze-dried. They have a mild and very aromatic flavor. So-called "pink pepper" is not really pepper at all, but a member of the elderberry family. The flavor is hot and peppery, with a hint of sweetness.
In order to retain both the spiciness and fragrance of pepper, grind the peppercorns over the food just before serving.

Rosemary

In appearance and aroma rosemary is rather similar to pine needles. It adds distinctive flavor fresh or

dried. The dry leaves remain fairly hard even when cooked. If this is not to your taste, you may prefer to crush them, using a pestle and mortar. Rosemary is good with all types of Mediterranean summer dishes, and is also delicious with pan-fried or roast potatoes.

Saffron

Since harvesting the delicate stigmas of the saffron crocus is done by hand, and is exceptionally laborious and not very productive, saffron is extremely expensive. There are many imitations on the market. You can avoid them to some extent by refusing to buy saffron in powdered form. Saffron has a strong smell and a slightly bitter taste. Used even in tiny quantities, it gives food a bright yellow color, making potato dishes look quite exotic.

Sage

The characteristic taste of the gray-green, silvery leaves gives any dish an "Italian" flavor. Crisply fried in hot fat, sage is particularly delicious. Try sprinkling it over pan-fried potatoes.

Savory

With a perfume similar to thyme, savory has a bitter, peppery flavor, which is most intense when the plant is just beginning to flower. It is then picked and dried. Savory is good in hearty potato soups and casseroles.

Thyme

The small thyme leaves have a powerful, slightly bitter taste, and do not lose any of their flavor when dried. In addition to common garden thyme, various types are grown for use in refined dishes, including lemon, orange, and caraway thyme. They provide novel flavors for potato dishes.

New Potatoes

For many of us the nicest thing about springtime is the arrival of new potatoes. While some people's thoughts immediately turn to asparagus, for others the best treat of all is a plateful of potatoes, with a little butter and salt, and nothing else.

New potatoes are sensitive creatures and must be handled with care. They should be neither peeled nor scrubbed, but simply rinsed under running water. With their paper-thin skins, they take less time to cook than older potatoes. Just place them in a pot of boiling water and they will be ready in an average of 15 minutes. The skin of new potatoes is a delicacy in itself. Although new potatoes have only a short season, it is best not to stock up on them, as their appearance soon spoils. Just buy them as you need them and enjoy them as fresh as possible.

Potatoes Provençal

3 ½ lb small new potatoes

6 tbsp olive oil

4 tbsp butter

salt

leaves from 3 stems of sage

leaves from 3 stems of marjoram

2 cloves garlic, chopped

2 tsp sugar

Leave the potatoes unpeeled and wash them clean, then dry thoroughly with paper towels.

Heat the olive oil in a heavy-based skillet, then lightly brown the potatoes, stirring constantly.

Reduce the heat and stir in the butter, salt, herbs and garlic.

Stirring constantly and shaking the skillet, fry the potatoes until golden brown.

The potatoes are done when they are tender enough to be pierced with a fork.

Sprinkle the sugar over the potatoes and cook until caramelized.

Season to taste with salt and serve piping hot.

Serves 4
227 calories per serving
Recommended salads: 5, 3

Asparagus and Prosciutto with Parsley Potatoes

4 ½ lb white asparagus
juice of 1 lemon
1 cup butter
1 tsp sugar
7 oz thinly sliced prosciutto

Peel the asparagus, cutting off the woody ends.

Bring a pot full of water to the boil with the lemon juice, butter and sugar.

Add the asparagus and cook for about 15 minutes.

Serve with prosciutto and new potatoes boiled in their skins and drenched in butter and finely chopped parsley.

Serves 4
625 calories per serving

Boiled Potatoes

For meat and fish dishes served with an exquisite sauce, there is no better accompaniment than boiled potatoes. Their velvety consistency enables them to absorb the sauce without impairing the flavor. Here is the best way to prepare boiled potatoes.

Peel the potatoes as thinly as possible, removing eyes and blemishes, then rinse and place them in cold salted water. The less water used, the more vitamins the potatoes will retain. As soon as the water comes to the boil, turn the heat down so that it is just enough to keep the pot bubbling. After 20 minutes, test the potatoes by piercing them with a fork or the point of a knife. If they are soft all the way through, then they are done. If necessary, for larger potatoes, cook for a few minutes longer. Drain off the water, then, leaving the lid off, return the pot to the heat and shake it gently a couple of times, making sure the potatoes do not burn.

Potatoes in Paradise

With only minimum effort, you can prepare
a meal like this to please even the most
demanding guest. First boil some really
good-quality potatoes in their skins, then
surround them with a selection of
ingredients, from the refined to the
substantial, from caviar to the humble
onion. Simply anything tastes wonderful
with potatoes boiled in their skins!

Clockwise:

Beluga caviar

Watercress

Cream cheese

Sevruga caviar

Scallion

Lime

Parsley

Hard-boiled egg

Chives

Onion

Butter

Crème fraîche

Salmon caviar

Radish

Smoked salmon

Dillweed

Herb butter

Rollmop herring

Recommended salad: 1

Potato Salads

Potato Salad with Bacon, Onions and Parsley

2 lb potatoes

7 oz slab smoked bacon

4 tbsp vinegar

12 tbsp oil

salt

freshly ground pepper

3 onions, diced

1 bunch parsley, finely chopped

Peel, boil and slice the potatoes.

Dice the bacon and fry it at a high heat until crispy.

Mix the vinegar, oil, salt and pepper together to make the marinade.

Carefully place the potato slices in the marinade.

Add the bacon and onions, and mix.

Serve garnished with parsley.

Serves 4
635 calories per serving

Potato Salad with Apples and Almonds

2 ¼ lb potatoes, boiled in their skins
2 white onions
¾ cup peeled almonds
1 lb red apples
juice of 1 lemon
2 egg yolks
½–1 cup walnut oil
½ cup heavy cream, whipped
2 tbsp apple juice
3 tbsp cider vinegar
salt
freshly ground pepper

Peel the potatoes while still warm, then slice.

Peel and slice the onions.

Halve the almonds and toast in a dry skillet.

Cut the apples into quarters, core, and sprinkle with lemon juice.

Beat the egg yolks until frothy, then gradually add the oil to make mayonnaise.

Fold in the cream, apple juice and vinegar, and season with salt and pepper.

Carefully mix the onions, almonds and apples, and toss in the mayonnaise.

Potato Salad with Cheese and Olives

2 ¼ lb potatoes, boiled in their skins	Peel the potatoes while still warm.
12 tbsp olive oil	Heat the olive oil in a skillet, and brown the rosemary and onions. Drain off and reserve the oil.
1 sprig rosemary	
1 white onion, finely chopped	
1 egg yolk	Beat the egg yolk until frothy, then add the oil a little at a time to make mayonnaise.
3 tbsp vinegar	
salt	Season to taste with vinegar, salt and pepper.
freshly ground pepper	
2 beefsteak tomatoes, skinned and deseeded	Dice the tomatoes, slice the potatoes and crumble the cheese.
1 ½ cup ewe's milk cheese	
½ cup black olives	Carefully stir the onions, tomatoes, olives, cheese and rosemary into the mayonnaise.
leaves of 1 sprig rosemary	
	Serve sprinkled with rosemary.

47

Pan-Fried Potatoes

Nearly every fried-potato fan has his or her own special recipe. Nevertheless, they all agree on a few ground rules. Baking potatoes are best, since they retain their shape. Do not use butter or virgin olive oil, as they cannot be heated to a high enough temperature. Neutral-tasting vegetable oil or fat, or clarified butter, is good for frying potatoes, and so are pork and goose dripping, if you like the taste.

Raw potatoes for frying should be sliced or diced. Heat the fat in the biggest available skillet. Add the potatoes and reduce the heat to medium. Pan-fried potatoes turn out best when they have plenty of room to move in the pan. They should not overlap. Most important of all: be patient! It takes at least 20 minutes to cook raw potatoes in a skillet to be sure they are tender and crunchy. Turn them over only when the underside is nice and crisp. Too much stirring and turning will only make them mushy and shapeless. Onions should be added to the skillet after about 10 minutes. Wait until the potatoes are done before sprinkling them with salt, pepper and herbs. For a touch of luxury, melt a generous pat of butter over them just before serving.

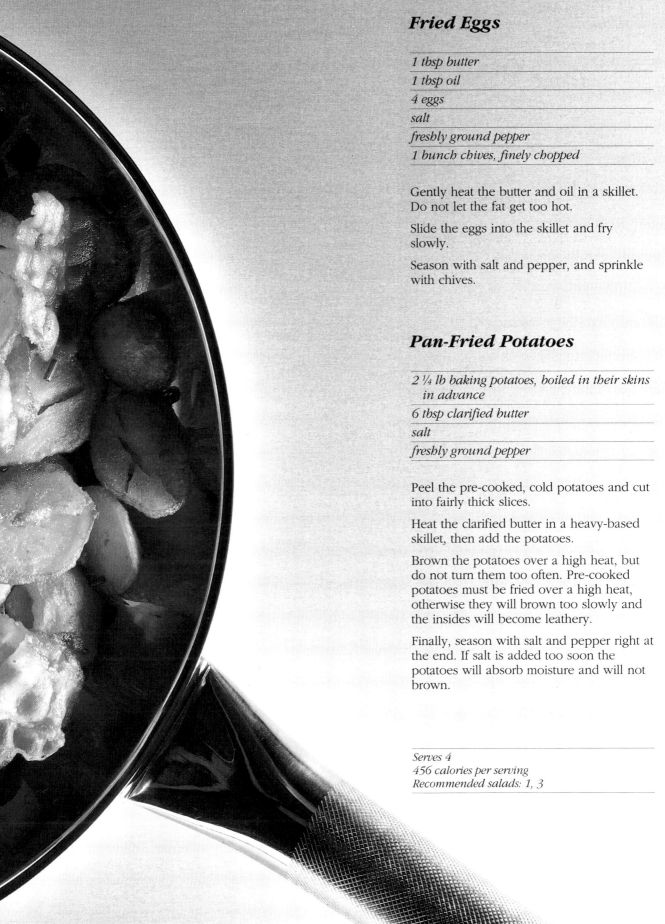

Fried Eggs

1 tbsp butter

1 tbsp oil

4 eggs

salt

freshly ground pepper

1 bunch chives, finely chopped

Gently heat the butter and oil in a skillet. Do not let the fat get too hot.

Slide the eggs into the skillet and fry slowly.

Season with salt and pepper, and sprinkle with chives.

Pan-Fried Potatoes

2 ¼ lb baking potatoes, boiled in their skins in advance

6 tbsp clarified butter

salt

freshly ground pepper

Peel the pre-cooked, cold potatoes and cut into fairly thick slices.

Heat the clarified butter in a heavy-based skillet, then add the potatoes.

Brown the potatoes over a high heat, but do not turn them too often. Pre-cooked potatoes must be fried over a high heat, otherwise they will brown too slowly and the insides will become leathery.

Finally, season with salt and pepper right at the end. If salt is added too soon the potatoes will absorb moisture and will not brown.

Serves 4
456 calories per serving
Recommended salads: 1, 3

Sausage Ring

1 tbsp butter

1 tbsp oil

1 large bratwurst or other sausage

Heat the butter and oil in a skillet.

Roll the sausage into a spiral and secure with a wooden skewer.

Add the sausage to the skillet.

Fry for about 5 minutes on each side.

Baste occasionally with fat.

Serve with Pan-Fried Potatoes.

Serves 4
133 calories per serving
Recommended salad: 3

Summer Vegetable Mold in Aspic with Cucumber

1 bunch white baby turnips
1 bunch spring carrots
1 lb broccoli
1 medium-sized cauliflower
½ lb green beans
4 tbsp gelatine
4 ½ cups strongly flavored instant vegetable stock
½ cup dry sherry
1 cucumber
1 tbsp butter
dillweed, finely chopped
½ cup white wine
salt
freshly ground pepper

Clean and peel the vegetables. Cut the turnips and carrots into strips. Divide the broccoli and cauliflower into flowerets. Cut the ends off the beans.

Cook the vegetables separately in salted water or steam until tender but still crisp. Drain in a colander and rinse under cold water. Dry thoroughly on paper towels.

Soak the gelatine in 8 tablespoons cold water for 4 minutes. Heat the stock and sherry, then dissolve the gelatine in the liquid.

Pour a little stock into a terrine dish. Place in the refrigerator until set. Add the carrots, then carefully cover with more stock. Repeat the process with each of the vegetables, allowing each layer to set before adding the next layer of vegetables.

Chill the terrine in the refrigerator for 5–6 hours.

Peel the cucumber and cut into sticks.

Heat the butter and sauté the cucumber. Add the dillweed and wine, and season to taste with salt and pepper.

Cut the mold into slices and serve with the cucumber and Pan-Fried Potatoes.

Serves 4
227 calories per serving
Recommended salads: 5, 3

Pot Roast with Vegetables

2 ¼ lb leg of beef

3–4 beef bones

1 bunch soup vegetables, such as leek, carrot and celery

1 tsp salt

1 peeled parsley root, if available

3 peppercorns

2 bay leaves

1 onion spiked with 4 cloves

2 leeks

1 bunch carrots

1 bunch white baby turnips

1 small head celeriac

Place the meat and bones in a large pot with enough cold water to cover. Bring to the boil over a medium heat, skimming off the scum.

Turn down the heat and add the soup vegetables, salt, parsley root, peppercorns, bay leaves and onion.

Simmer gently for 3 hours.

Leave the meat to cool in the broth, then strain the broth, reserving it and the meat separately.

Trim and wash the leek and carrots. Peel the turnips and the celeriac. Cut the leek diagonally into pieces. Cut the celeriac into eight sections. Leave the carrots and turnips whole.

Add the vegetables to the broth and cook for 20 minutes until tender.

Thinly slice the beef and serve with the vegetables and Pan-Fried Potatoes.

Optional

Freshly grated horseradish

Apple and horseradish sauce (a mixture of equal quantities of grated apple and horseradish)

Chive sauce (crème fraîche mixed with chives and seasoned with salt and pepper)

Serves 4
299 calories per serving
Recommended salad: 6

Veal in Mushroom Sauce

1 ¼ lb thin veal scallops
2 tbsp oil
2 tbsp butter
1 onion, finely chopped
3 ½ cups button mushrooms, thinly sliced
1 bunch tarragon, finely chopped
1 cup white wine
1 cup light cream
salt
freshly ground pepper

Cut the scallops into thin strips about 2 ½ inches long.

Heat the oil in a skillet, and brown the meat in batches. Drain the meat through a sieve, reserving the juices.

Heat the butter in the skillet, and sauté the onion and mushrooms. Stir in the tarragon. Add the wine, bring to the boil and reduce the liquid slightly. Add the cream and meat juices, then reduce to a creamy sauce.

Return the meat to the skillet and heat through. Season to taste with salt and pepper.

Serve the veal with wedges of Hash Brown Potatoes.

Hash Brown Potatoes

1 ¾ lb potatoes boiled in their skins the day before
salt
3 tbsp oil
3 tbsp butter

Peel the potatoes, grate coarsely, and season with salt.

Heat the oil and butter in a non-stick skillet, add the potatoes and fry over a medium heat until golden, pressing the potatoes flat in the skillet.

Cover the potatoes with a plate, turn the skillet and plate upside down, then slide the potatoes back into the skillet. Fry the other side until crisp and golden.

Serves 4
588 calories per serving

Potato and Onion Omelet

7 oz onions

14 oz potatoes

6 tbsp olive oil

salt

freshly ground pepper

6 eggs

Peel and dice the onions.

Peel the potatoes and cut into 1-inch cubes.

Heat 4 tablespoons of the oil in a skillet and fry the onions until transparent.

Add the potatoes and cook for about 15 minutes until soft, turning occasionally.

Season with salt and pepper.

Beat the eggs until frothy, add salt and pour over the potatoes. Allow to thicken, turning frequently. Place a lid on the skillet and cook on a low heat until golden yellow, shaking occasionally.

Cover the omelet with a plate and turn it and the skillet upside-down. Place the remaining oil in the skillet, slide the omelet into it and cook on a low heat, with the lid off, until golden.

Serves 4
242 calories per serving
Recommended salad: 4

Soups

Creamy, textured potato soups are traditional favorites. Now the latest invention and a small culinary miracle, clear potato soup is a perfect example of the versatility of the potato. If you are serving potato soup as an appetizer, use only the finest ingredients, as illustrated in the following pages.

Potato Consommé with Crayfish

12 crayfish

1 zucchini

1 red radish

2 carrots

2 tomatoes, peeled and deseeded

2 ¼ lb potatoes

2 tbsp oil

4 ½ cups beef consommé

salt

freshly ground pepper

leaves of 2 sprigs basil

Simmer the crayfish in boiling salted water for 4 minutes.

Drain in a colander, allow to cool, then remove the shells.

Trim and wash the zucchini, radish and carrots, then cut them into finger-length sticks. Dice the tomatoes.

Peel the potatoes, slice half of them, and cut the rest into thin strips. Cook the vegetables and potatoes separately until tender but still crisp, drain in a colander and rinse under cold running water.

Heat the oil in a skillet and fry the sliced potatoes until crisp and brown.

Add the beef consommé and simmer gently for 10 minutes.

Strain through a sieve and season to taste with salt and pepper.

Add the potato strips and vegetable strips to the soup, then reheat gently.

Divide the crayfish between 4 plates, and pour the soup over them.

Serve garnished with basil leaves.

Serves 4
440 calories per serving

63

German-Style Potato Soup

2 ¼ lb potatoes

7 tbsp butter

¼ head of celeriac, diced

1 diced carrot

1 leek, cut lengthwise into strips, then sliced crosswise

1 diced onion

1 cup light cream

salt

freshly ground pepper

nutmeg

4 slices white bread

3 ½ oz slab smoked bacon

1 fresh garlic stalk or 1 scallion, cut diagonally into thin strips

Peel and coarsely dice the potatoes

Heat 4 tablespoons of the butter in a large saucepan. Sauté the potatoes, celeriac and carrots in the butter, then cover with cold water.

Simmer over a low heat for 40 minutes.

Pass half the soup through a sieve, mashing the potatoes and vegetables to a purée. Heat 1 tablespoon of butter in a skillet and sauté the leek and onion, add to the purée, then combine with the rest of the soup.

Add the cream and simmer for about 5 minutes, then season to taste with salt, pepper and nutmeg.

To make croûtons, dice the bread, heat the remaining butter in a skillet and fry the bread until golden brown.

Dice the bacon and brown in the butter-coated skillet.

Serve the soup sprinkled with croûtons, diced bacon and garlic stalk or scallion.

Serves 4
670 calories per serving

Potato Soup with Truffles

1 lb potatoes
1 cup light cream
1 cup butter
salt
freshly ground pepper
nutmeg
2 ½ cups highly seasoned beef consommé
3 ½ oz black or white truffles
leaves from 1 sprig watercress or purslane

Peel 12 oz potatoes, cook in salted water for about 20 minutes, then drain in a colander.

Mash them to a smooth purée with the cream and half the butter.

Season with salt, pepper and nutmeg. Add the consommé and bring to the boil. Stir thoroughly with a whisk.

Peel and finely dice the remaining potatoes.

Clarify the rest of the butter. When the butter is hot, fry the potatoes until crisp.

Scrub the truffles clean.

Add the fried potatoes to the soup and reheat gently.

Serve garnished with finely sliced truffles and watercress or purslane leaves.

Serves 4
620 calories per serving

Potato and Watercress Soup

1 lb potatoes
1 cup chicken stock
1 cup heavy cream, stiffly whipped
salt
freshly ground pepper
7 tbsp butter
1 onion, finely chopped
1 bunch watercress, finely chopped

Peel the potatoes and cut them into chunks. Cook in salted water for about 15 minutes, then drain in a colander.

Mash the potatoes, then add the chicken stock and stir thoroughly.

Fold in the whipped cream and season to taste with salt and pepper.

Heat the butter in a skillet, sauté the onion and watercress, and add them to the soup.

Purée the soup in a blender.

Gently heat through again.

Serves 4
460 calories per serving

One-Pot Meals

There is nothing quite so satisfying as chunky stews and casseroles. These sturdier members of the soup family are packed with goodness. When temperatures start to fall outside, they really come into their own, with hearty ingredients to warm both heart and stomach. You can use any kind of meat, especially smoked specialities, which add extra flavor, but what makes theses one-pot meals so smoothly satisfying is the essential ingredient: potatoes.

Bacon, Pork and Potato Casserole

3 ½ lb potatoes

2 large onions

1 lb thin-sliced smoked bacon

1 lb unsmoked belly of pork

freshly ground pepper

2 ½ cups light cream

1 cup white wine

pinch of cinnamon

7 tbsp butter, chilled and flaked

salt

Peel the potatoes and cut into slices ½ inch thick.

Peel and slice the onions.

Remove any rind from the bacon. Line the base of a saucepan or casserole dish suitable for use on the stove with the bacon. Add the potatoes and onions.

Score a crisscross pattern in the pork rind, and season with pepper. Add to the potatoes and onions. Pour on the cream and wine.

Sprinkle with cinnamon and flakes of butter.

Place the lid on the pot, then simmer gently for 1–1 ½ hours without stirring.

Season to taste with salt and pepper.

Serves 4
194 calories per serving

Beef and Pork Stew

14 oz leg of beef

14 oz leg of pork

2 ¼ lb potatoes

4 tbsp oil

salt

freshly ground pepper

½ head celeriac, peeled and diced

1 bunch carrots, diced

1 leek, cut lengthwise into strips, then sliced crosswise

¼ lb green beans

2 ½ cups chicken stock

1 bunch parsley, finely chopped

Cut the meat into ½-inch cubes. Peel the potatoes and cut them into ½-inch cubes.

Heat the oil and fry the meat until browned all over. Season with salt and pepper.

Line the base of a large saucepan with a layer of potatoes and vegetables, then cover with a layer of meat. Continue to add alternate layers of meat and vegetables, ending with a layer of vegetables.

Pour in the chicken stock, place the lid on the pot and simmer gently for about 60 minutes.

Season to taste with salt and pepper, then serve sprinkled with chopped parsley.

Serves 4
753 calories per serving

Sausage, Leek and Potato Hotpot

2 ¼ lb potatoes

4 leeks

3 tbsp butter

1 large onion, finely chopped

leaves from 1 bunch marjoram

3 cups chicken stock

salt

8 boiling sausages

1 bunch parsley, finely chopped

Peel and dice the potatoes.

Using only the white parts of the leeks, cut in half lengthwise, then thickly slice them crosswise.

Heat the butter in a large saucepan and sauté the onions and potatoes in it.

Add the leeks, marjoram and salt, and pour in the stock.

Simmer gently for about 40 minutes.

Add the sausages, then simmer for a further 15 minutes.

Serve sprinkled with parsley.

Serves 4
535 calories per serving

Potato Purées

Children love potato purées, but adults too should indulge in them more often. This is the best way to prepare them: peel and boil the potatoes.(You can boil them in their skins, but they will cool down too much while you peel them.) To mash the potatoes, use a potato press or pass them through a sieve with a potato masher, using firm, downward (not sideways) movements. Never use a blender or food processor: the swift circular movement extracts too much starch from the potatoes, making the purée transparent and sticky. Whether you prefer your purée completely smooth or with a few solid bits is purely a matter of individual taste. When the purée is the right consistency, gradually add boiling milk, then stir slowly with a hand whisk, until light and fluffy. At this point, season with salt, white pepper and grated nutmeg or mace. Finally, add a few flakes of butter, or a little melted butter, then serve on warm plates. Potato purée is at its best when fresh and hot!

Colorful Purées

Basic recipe

18 oz potatoes
½ cup hot milk
salt
freshly ground pepper
nutmeg
4 tbsp butter

Peel the potatoes and boil them in salted water for about 20 minutes.

Drain through a colander and leave to cool for a minute or two.

Mash the potatoes until smooth, add the milk and stir thoroughly with a hand whisk.

Season to taste with salt, pepper and nutmeg.

Fold in the butter.

Serves 4
202 calories per serving

Cèpe potato purée

1 cup (2 oz) dried cèpes
½ cup water
2 ¼ cups potato purée
salt
freshly ground pepper
nutmeg

Soak the cèpes in the water for 20 minutes, then remove, squeeze dry and chop finely.

Strain the cèpe water through a sieve, then boil over a high heat until reduced by half.

Stir the mushrooms and water into the hot potato purée, and season to taste with salt, pepper and nutmeg.

Serves 4
110 calories per serving

Beet potato purée

4 tbsp butter

½ cup hot beet juice

2 ¼ cups potato purée

salt

freshly ground pepper

Stir the butter and beet juice into the hot potato purée, and season to taste with salt and pepper.

Herb potato purée

small bunch chives, finely chopped

small bunch parsley, finely chopped

½ cup chervil, finely chopped

(add other herbs, if you like)

2 ¼ cups potato purée

4 tbsp butter

salt

freshly ground pepper

nutmeg

Add the herbs to the hot potato purée and stir thoroughly. Beat in the butter.

Season to taste with salt, pepper and nutmeg.

Saffron potato purée

4 tbsp butter

2 ¼ cups potato purée

4 g saffron

½ cup milk

salt

freshly ground pepper

Stir the butter into the potato purée.

Add the saffron to the milk, and bring briefly to the boil.

Stir the milk into the purée.

Season to taste with salt and pepper.

Serves 4
211 calories per serving

Serves 4
204 calories per serving

Serves 4
205 calories per serving

Turbot with Saffron Sauce and Beet Potato Purée

4 small turbot fillets
salt
freshly ground pepper
1 tbsp butter
1 shallot, finely chopped
½ cup white wine
4 g saffron
½ cup crème fraîche
½ cup heavy cream, stiffly whipped

Season the fish with salt and pepper.

Grease a saucepan with butter. Sprinkle the chopped shallot over the base of the pot and arrange the fish fillets on top.

Add the wine and place the lid on the pot. Bring to the boil over a high heat, then turn the heat down low and simmer for 3 minutes.

Remove the fish from the pot and keep warm.

Add the saffron to the fish stock, then boil over a high heat until the liquid is reduced by one-third. Add the crème fraîche and reduce the sauce by half.

Carefully fold in the whipped cream, and season to taste with salt and pepper.

Serve the fish with the saffron sauce and Beet Potato Purée.

Serves 4
671 calories per serving

"Heaven and Earth": Potatoes and Apples with Blood Pudding

3 ½ lb potatoes

½ cup light cream

10 tbsp butter

1 egg yolk

salt

freshly ground pepper

nutmeg

3 tbsp oil

1 blood pudding ring

2 large onions, sliced

3 unpeeled, sliced apples

1 tbsp flour

Peel the potatoes, cut them into chunks and boil for about 20 minutes.

Drain in a colander and leave to cool for a few minutes.

Mash the potatoes until smooth.

Bring the cream and 7 tablespoons of butter to the boil, then stir into the purée. Add the egg yolk.

Season to taste with salt, pepper and nutmeg.

Heat the oil in a skillet. Fry the blood pudding for about 10 minutes, turning frequently.

Heat half the remaining butter, then fry the onions until golden brown.

Coat the apple slices in flour.

Heat the rest of the butter and fry the apple until golden brown.

Cut the blood pudding into eight pieces, and arrange with the onions and apples on top of the purée.

Serves 4
832 calories per serving

Duck Breast with Shallot Butter

4 duck breasts
1 tbsp oil
9 tbsp butter
salt
freshly ground pepper
4 shallots, finely chopped
1 ½ cups red wine

Pat the duck breasts dry with paper towels.

Heat the oil and 1 tablespoon of the butter in a casserole and sear the duck breasts.

Season with salt and pepper, and roast in an oven at 400°F for 10–15 minutes, depending on size, until pink, basting frequently.

Remove, wrap in aluminum foil and leave for 5 minutes,

Pour off the fat from the casserole, add 1 tablespoon butter and fry the shallots. Chill the remaining butter.

Add the red wine and cook on a high heat until the liquid has reduced by two-thirds.

Make the sauce by adding pieces of the chilled butter while beating constantly with a whisk.

Thinly slice the duck breasts and serve with the sauce.

Duchess Potatoes

2 ¼ lb potatoes
½ cup light cream
2 egg yolks
salt
freshly ground pepper
a little oil
nutmeg

Peel the potatoes, cut them into halves and boil in salted water for about 20 minutes.

Pour into a colander and allow to cool slightly.

Mash the potatoes.

Heat the cream and mix with the potatoes.

Add the egg yolks and stir well.

Season with salt, pepper and nutmeg.

Place in an pastry bag with a large star-shaped tip.

Grease a baking sheet with oil and squeeze small rosettes on to it.

Brown in an oven for 10–12 minutes at 400°F.

Serves 4
736 calories per serving
Recommended salad: 2

Dumplings

Potatoes are ideal for making dumplings. You must be patient, since the round potato balls do not always come out perfectly at the first attempt. They may be as hard as tennis balls, or they may fall apart as they cook. You need to have taken a course in body-building to prepare dumplings using raw potatoes, while kneading the dough for boiled dumplings requires the lightest of touches. Even then, the result will be only as good as the basic ingredient: potatoes. The first step is to find potatoes of the right fluffy texture. Then have confidence in your own skill and in the tried and tested recipes on the following pages.

The Perfect Dumplings

5 slices white bread, crusts removed
4 tbsp oil
3 lb large potatoes
½ cup milk
⅓ cup semolina
1 ¾ cups all-purpose flour
1–2 tsp salt
nutmeg

Dice the bread. Heat the oil in a skillet and fry until golden brown.

Peel the potatoes and grate, using the serrated side of the grater.

Wrap the grated potatoes in a dish towel and squeeze out thoroughly.

Place the potatoes in water, drain and then wring out again (they must be very dry).

Bring the milk and semolina to the boil, then stir in the potatoes.

Add the flour and beat vigorously, then knead to a dough.

Season with salt and nutmeg.

With wet hands, shape the dough into large round dumplings. Add about 3 bread dice to each dumpling and place in a saucepan with boiling salted water.

Reduce the heat and cook the dumplings in gently bubbling water for about 40 minutes.

Serves 4
572 calories per serving

Breast of Goose with Red Cabbage

2 medium-sized goose breasts

salt

freshly ground pepper

½ cup butter

2 tbsp oil

1 finely chopped duck carcass, if available

1 bunch soup vegetables, such as leek, carrot and celery, finely chopped

3 tbsp all-purpose flour

1 cup red wine

1 cup water, or chicken stock if duck carcass not used

10 white peppercorns

1 tbsp crème fraîche

1 tbsp goose or duck fat

1 Spanish onion, finely chopped

3 cups canned red cabbage

½ cup apple cider

1 russet apple

1 tbsp apple jelly

Season the goose breasts with salt and pepper.

Heat 1 ½ tablespoons of the butter and the oil in a roasting pan, and fry the goose breasts until golden brown. Put the remaining butter in the refrigerator.

Add the carcass and chopped vegetables, and brown briefly.

Preheat the oven to 400°F and roast the goose breasts and vegetables in the oven for 20–30 minutes, basting frequently with the pan juices.

Remove the goose from the pan, wrap in aluminum foil and keep warm.

Sprinkle the carcass and vegetables with flour, pour in the wine and water or stock, then add the peppercorns.

Reduce the liquid by half over a high heat.

Strain the sauce through a sieve, then simmer for a further 5 minutes. In the meantime, take the butter out of the refrigerator and cut it into pieces.

Using a whisk, beat the butter into the sauce, then season to taste with salt and pepper.

Stir in the crème fraîche.

Heat the goose or duck fat in a saucepan, and sauté the onions in it.

Add the red cabbage, stir thoroughly and pour in the cider.

Cook over a low heat for 10 minutes.

Core and quarter the apple, then cut it into thin wedges.

Add to the red cabbage and cook for a further 20 minutes, until tender.

Season with apple jelly, salt and pepper.

Serve the goose with the red cabbage and sauce.

Serve with Perfect Dumplings

Serves 4
463 calories per serving

Fillets of Sole

12 sole fillets

1 tbsp butter

2 shallots, finely chopped

salt

freshly ground pepper

½ cup white wine

1 cup crème fraîche

5 tbsp freshly grated horseradish

⅔ cup cooked, peeled shrimp

small bunch sorrel, finely chopped

Flatten the sole fillets with a knife, then roll them up.

Grease a saucepan with the butter, add the shallots and season with salt and pepper.

Add the rolled fish fillets and pour in the wine. Place the lid on the saucepan, bring to the boil, then cook over a low heat for about 2 minutes.

Remove the fish from the pan and keep warm.

Strain the stock.

Over a high heat, reduce the liquid by one-third. Add the crème fraîche and reduce by three-quarters.

Stir the horseradish into the sauce. Add the rolled fish fillets and shrimp and gently heat through for about a minute, then add the sorrel.

Serve the fish with sauce and Soufflé Dumplings.

Soufflé Dumplings

1 ⅔ lb potatoes, boiled in their skins

1 egg yolk

½ cup heavy cream, whipped

6 tbsp all-purpose flour

3 egg whites, stiffly beaten

salt

nutmeg

Boil the potatoes, then peel and allow to cool.

Rub through a sieve, then stir in the egg yolk and cream.

Stir in the flour.

Carefully fold in half the beaten egg white, then gradually add the rest. Season with salt and nutmeg.

Take soup-spoonfuls of dough and place them in boiling salted water and simmer over a low heat for about 20 minutes.

Serves 4
380 calories per serving

Apricot Dumplings with Poppy Seeds

2 ¼ lb potatoes, boiled in their skins

1–2 eggs

1 ¼ cups all-purpose flour

8 apricots

8 cubes sugar

4 tbsp butter

3 tbsp poppy seeds

2 tbsp granulated sugar

½ tbsp ground cinnamon

Peel the boiled potatoes while still warm, then mash until smooth.

Add the eggs, stirring vigorously.

Stir in the flour.

Stone the apricots, cutting larger ones in half.

Shape the dough into dumplings the size of a tennis ball, press 1 apricot and a cube of sugar into each dumpling.

Mold the dumplings to a nice round shape, then place in lightly salted, boiling water and simmer over a low heat for about 20 minutes.

Melt the butter in a small saucepan, then stir in the poppy seeds and granulated sugar.

Remove the dumplings from the water, and drain briefly.

Sprinkle with cinnamon and pour the poppy-seed sauce on top.

Serves 4
539 calories per serving

Cinnamon Dumplings

1 ¼ lb potatoes

1 tbsp butter

2 ½ cups milk

½ cup sugar

1 tbsp cinnamon

⅔ cup semolina

2 eggs

butter for frying

Peel the potatoes, cut into large chunks and boil in salted water for about 20 minutes.

Drain in a sieve and allow to cool for 1–2 minutes. Rub through the sieve, then stir in the butter.

Bring the milk to the boil with the sugar and cinnamon, then slowly trickle the semolina into the saucepan.

Remove from the heat, beat in the eggs, and stir thoroughly.

While still hot, add the semolina mixture to the potatoes, mix together thoroughly and leave to cool.

Gently melt the butter in a skillet.

Take soup-spoonfuls of dough and slide them into the hot butter. Fry until golden brown all over.

Serve with the Fruit Compote.

Fruit Compote

3 canned pears

1 papaya

½ cup syrup from the pears

16 canned or bottled crab apples, or, if unavailable, canned or bottled lychees or kumquats

2 tsp Cointreau

1 orange

½ tsp cinnamon

7 tbsp butter, chilled and flaked.

Slice the pears. Peel the papaya, then cut into balls with a melon baller.

Pour the pear syrup into a saucepan and lightly warm the preserved crab apples, pears and papaya in it. Remove the fruit from the pot. Add the Cointreau to the syrup and reduce the liquid by two-thirds.

Wash the orange, and cut the peel into julienne strips. Add the peel and cinnamon to the syrup.

Stir the butter into the syrup.

Return the fruit to the pot and gently warm through.

Serves 4
831 calories per serving

Fillet of Venison

2 tbsp oil

1 lb chopped venison bones

1 bunch soup vegetables, such as leek,
carrot and celery , finely chopped

1 cup white wine

1 cup water

1 cup freshly squeezed orange juice

4 oranges

10 tbsp butter, straight from the
refrigerator, cut into small pieces

1 ⅔ lb boned saddle of venison

4 tbsp butter

salt

freshly ground pepper

Heat 1 tablespoon of the oil in a saucepan, and brown the venison bones and soup vegetables.

Pour in the wine and water, and reduce the liquid by half over a medium heat.

Rub through a sieve, then reduce the stock by one-quarter over a low heat.

Add the orange juice and again reduce by half.

Wash 1 orange, cut the peel into julienne strips, add to the sauce and simmer for 1–2 minutes.

Peel the other 3 oranges, remove the pith and cut all 4 oranges into thin segments.

Stir the chilled butter into the sauce, season with salt and pepper, and add some of the orange segments.

Season the venison with salt and pepper.

Heat 4 tablespoons of butter and the remaining oil in a roasting pan and brown the meat all over. Roast in the oven at 400˚F for 8–10 minutes, turning frequently.

Remove the meat from the oven, wrap in aluminum foil and leave to stand for 5 minutes.

Slice the meat, decorate with orange segments, and serve with the sauce and Mushroom Dumplings.

Mushroom Dumplings

4 ½ cups mixed mushrooms (such as
button mushrooms, cèpes, shitake)

1 tbsp butter

1 shallot, finely chopped

salt

14 oz raw potatoes

14 oz potatoes, boiled in their skins

1 cup all-purpose flour

½ cup hot milk

2 eggs

Trim the mushrooms, wash very briefly, pat dry and chop finely.

Heat the butter in a skillet, sauté the shallot, then add the mushrooms.

Fry for about 3 minutes until transparent, then season with salt.

Peel and grate the raw potatoes.

Wrap the grated potatoes in a dish towel and squeeze thoroughly.

Peel and grate the cooked potatoes and mix with the raw potatoes.

Add the flour and stir thoroughly.

Stir in the milk.

Add the eggs and continue to stir.

Mix in the chopped mushrooms.

With wet hands, shape the dough into eight dumplings. Place in a saucepan of boiling water, reduce the heat and simmer for about 20–25 minutes.

Serves 4
507 calories per serving
Recommended salad: 4

Gnocchi

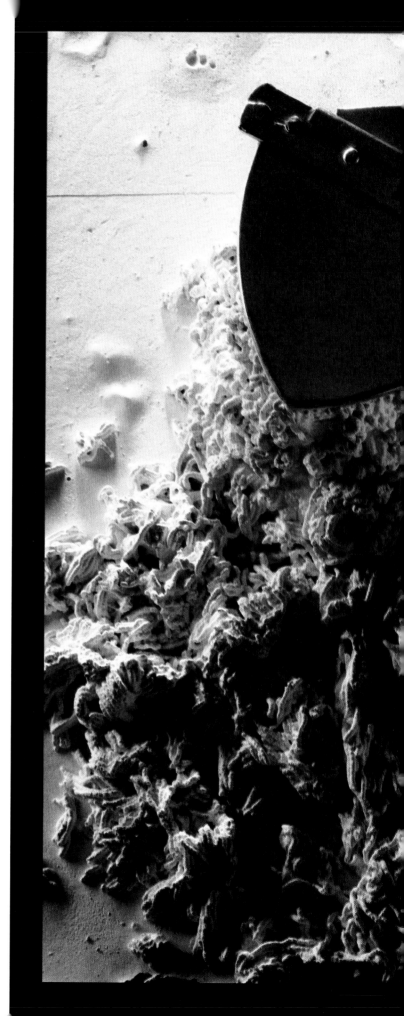

For fans of Italian food, potato
dumplings should be on the
smaller side – preferably in the
form of gnocchi. These are made
from the same basic ingredients,
although there are also gnocchi
using semolina or flour. The
shape of the gnocchi is important:
use your thumb to make a nice
deep hollow in the middle of each
potato roll. This enables the
gnocchi on the plate to soak up
lots of sauce or sage butter. If you
like your gnocchi saucier still,
press the back of a fork into the
dough, creating more grooves
and making the gnocchi more
absorbent.

102

Gnocchi with Tomato Sauce and Parmesan Cheese

2 ¼ lb potatoes, boiled in their skins
2 eggs
1 ¼–2 ¼ cups all-purpose flour
salt
8 tbsp olive oil
1 onion, finely chopped
4 cloves of garlic, finely chopped
4 cups canned tomatoes
1 sprig basil
1 cup grated Parmesan cheese
leaves from 1 bunch of basil
freshly ground pepper
sugar

Peel the boiled potatoes while still warm, then mash them until smooth.

Add the eggs and mix thoroughly.

Knead in enough flour to make a firm, workable dough.

Season with salt.

Roll out the potato dough on a floured wooden board until it is the thickness of a finger. Cut into pieces ½ inches wide and 2 inches long.

Roll the pieces into little sausage shapes. Using your thumb, press a hollow in each shape.

Place the gnocchi in a pot of boiling water and simmer over a low heat for 4–6 minutes, then drain through a sieve.

Heat 5 tablespoons of the olive oil in a saucepan, and sauté the onions and garlic in it.

Add the tomatoes and sprig of basil, and simmer for about 30 minutes.

Stir occasionally with a whisk to break up the tomatoes.

Season with salt, pepper and sugar.

Grease a warmed serving bowl with the remaining olive oil and add the gnocchi.

Pour on the tomato sauce and sprinkle with Parmesan cheese.

Sprinkle with basil and serve.

Serves 4
554 calories per serving

Spinach Gnocchi and Ricotta Cheese Bake

2 ¼ lb potatoes, boiled in their skins

2 eggs

1 cup butter

3 cloves garlic, finely chopped

1 ⅔ lb (20 cups) washed and trimmed spinach

2–2 ¼ cups all-purpose flour

salt

1 ¼ cups ricotta cheese

Peel the boiled potatoes while still warm, then mash them until smooth.

Add the eggs and mix thoroughly.

Heat half the butter in a large saucepan, sauté the garlic, then add half the spinach and cook for 3 minutes.

Finely chop or purée the rest of the spinach and stir into the mashed potatoes.

Knead in enough flour to make a firm, workable dough.

Season with salt.

Roll out the potato dough on a floured wooden board until it is as thick as a finger. Cut into pieces ½ inches wide and 2 inches long.

Roll the pieces into little sausage shapes. Using your thumb, press a hollow in each shape.

Transfer the gnocchi to a pot of boiling water and simmer over a low heat for 4–6 minutes, then drain through a sieve.

Place the gnocchi in an ovenproof dish, stir in the rest of the spinach and crumble the ricotta cheese over the top.

Melt the remaining butter and pour over the gnocchi.

Bake in the oven at 400˚F for 5–8 minutes until the cheese melts.

Serves 4
1121 calories per serving

Fritters and Crêpes

Potato Fritters

2 ¼ lb potatoes
3 scallions
1 egg
2 tbsp all-purpose flour
salt
oil for frying

Wash, peel and finely grate the potatoes.

Cut the white and pale green parts of the scallions into thin rings.

Stir the egg and flour into the grated potatoes. Season with salt, and fold in the scallions.

Heat the oil in a skillet.

Take soup-spoonfuls of the mixture and carefully slide them into the hot oil, flattening them slightly. Fry until a light golden brown on both sides.

Serves 4
240 calories per serving

Herb Potato Fritters

1 ½ lb potatoes
1 tbsp butter
1 egg
3 tbsp all-purpose flour
small bunch parsley, finely chopped
small bunch basil, finely chopped
salt
freshly ground pepper
oil for frying

Peel the potatoes and cut into chunks. Cook in salted water for about 20 minutes, then drain in a sieve. Rub them through the sieve while still warm.

Stir in the butter. Add the egg, flour, parsley and basil, and stir thoroughly. Season with salt and pepper.

Heat the oil in a skillet and cook as above.

Serves 4
173 calories per serving

Quail Breasts

4 quail

salt

2 tbsp oil

1 sprig rosemary

½ cup apple juice

½ cup white wine

3 tbsp honey

4 tbsp butter, straight from the
   refrigerator and cut into small pieces

freshly ground pepper

4 zucchini flowers

Season the quail with salt.

Heat the oil in a heat-proof casserole, and
brown the quail all over.

Transfer the quail to the oven and cook at
400°F for 10 minutes.

Remove the quail from the oven, wrap in
aluminum foil and keep warm.

Pour off the fat, reheat the casserole and
sauté the rosemary.

Add the apple juice, bring to the boil, then
pour in the wine.

Reduce the liquid by half, stir in the honey
and return to the boil.

Stir the butter into the sauce.

Discard the rosemary and season the sauce
with salt and pepper.

Add the zucchini flowers and simmer for a
further 4 minutes.

Unwrap the quail breasts and serve with
the zucchini flowers, sauce and Herb
Potato Fritters.

Serves 4
288 calories per serving

110

Langoustine in Mushroom Sauce with Potato Fritters

2 tbsp butter

1 onion, finely chopped

4–7 cups mixed mushrooms (such as shitake, button mushrooms, oyster mushrooms)

½ cup crème fraîche

1 cooked langoustine

leaves of 1 bunch basil, cut into strips

salt

freshly ground pepper

Heat the butter in a skillet and sauté the onion.

Clean the mushrooms, discarding the stalks if you prefer, and add to the onions.

When the mushrooms are glazed, add the crème fraîche and simmer gently for 5 minutes.

Break the langoustine into pieces and cut the tail into not-too-thick slices. Add to the mushroom sauce and heat through gently.

Season to taste with salt and pepper.

Sprinkle with basil and serve with Potato Fritters.

Serves 4
112 calories per serving

Potato Blinis

2 ¼ cups all-purpose flour

2 tbsp (2 packages) active dry yeast

1 tsp sugar

½ cup lukewarm milk

7 oz potatoes

1 tsp salt

1 egg

4 tbsp butter, melted

fat for frying

Sift the flour into a bowl.

Dissolve the yeast and sugar in some of the milk.

Make a well in the sifted flour and pour in the yeast mixture.

Cover the yeast mixture with flour, then leave to prove in a warm place for 20 minutes.

Wash and peel the potatoes, then boil in salted water for about 20 minutes.

Drain in a sieve, allow to cool a little, then rub through the sieve.

Add the salt to the flour and knead to a dough.

Stir the egg and butter into the mashed potatoes. Add the potatoes to the dough and knead thoroughly.

Leave the dough to prove for a further 20 minutes.

Heat the fat in a skillet. Take soup-spoonfuls of dough and carefully slide them into the hot fat, flattening them slightly.

Fry until the blinis are a light golden brown on both sides.

Smoked Salmon with Caviar and Quail Eggs

8 quail eggs

1 cup crème fraîche

2 limes (slice ½ lime, and squeeze the juice from the rest)

salt

freshly ground pepper

small bunch dillweed, finely chopped

14 oz thinly sliced smoked salmon

3 tbsp caviar

leaves from 2 stems of dillweed

Boil the quail eggs for 4 minutes, rinse in cold water, and shell.

Mix the crème fraîche with the lime juice, salt, pepper and dillweed, adjusting the seasoning as necessary.

Arrange the Potato Blinis on individual plates, and spread with crème fraîche.

Arrange the smoked salmon, caviar, quail eggs and lime slices on and around the blinis. Serve sprinkled with dillweed.

Serves 4
797 calories per serving

Fruit-Filled Crêpes

½ lb potatoes

4 eggs

1 cup all-purpose flour

½–1 cup milk

salt

a little oil

fruit filling (see opposite)

confectioner's sugar

Peel, boil and mash the potatoes.

Mix the eggs into the potatoes.

Sieve the flour into the mixture and stir.

Stir in enough milk to make a runny batter.

Add a pinch of salt and leave for 10 minutes.

Heat a little oil in a skillet.

Ladle the batter into the skillet and spread very thinly and evenly.

Fry until bubbles form on the surface and the edges look dry, then turn and cook the other side until golden brown.

Slide on to a plate, cover half the crêpe with fruit filling and fold over the other half.

Sprinkle with confectioner's sugar and serve.

Serves 4

295 calories per serving

1

1 small melon	
1 papaya	
2 tbsp Grand Marnier	
1 tbsp confectioner's sugar	

Peel the melon and make into balls with a melon baller. Peel the papaya and cut into pieces. Mix the two with Grand Marnier and confectioner's sugar, and leave for 30 minutes.

2

1 ⅓ cups raspberries	
1 ¾ cups blackberries	
2 tbsp kirsch	
2 tbsp confectioner's sugar	

Mix the berries with the kirsch and the confectioner's sugar, and leave for 30 minutes.

3

1 ⅔ cups strawberries	
1 tbsp confectioner's sugar	
1 cup heavy cream	
1 tbsp granulated sugar	

Slice the strawberries, mix with the confectioner's sugar and leave for 30 minutes. Beat the cream until stiff and sugar to taste. Combine the strawberries and cream.

4

2 oranges	
½ cup port	
3 tbsp granulated sugar	
4 figs	

Wash one of the oranges and finely grate the peel. Peel both oranges, separate into segments and remove the pips.Place the grated peel and segments in a saucepan with the port and sugar, and bring to the boil. Reduce heat, add the figs and simmer for 10 minutes until soft.

Potato Waffles

9 oz potatoes
2 ¼ cups all-purpose flour
1 ¼ cups confectioner's sugar
1 cup milk
⅔ cup coconut flakes
3 egg whites, stiffly beaten
oil for greasing

Wash and peel the potatoes, then cut into chunks.

Boil in lightly salted water for about 15 minutes.

Drain in a colander and leave to cool a little.

Mash the potatoes and sift the flour on top.

Add the confectioner's sugar and milk and stir to a smooth batter.

Stir in the coconut flakes.

Carefully fold in the egg whites.

Heat the waffle iron and brush lightly with oil.

Using a small ladle, pour the batter into the waffle iron and cook until the waffles are a light golden brown.

Serve with blackcurrant ice cream and Redcurrant Compote, or lemon ice cream and Apple Compote.

Serves 4
502 calories per serving

Redcurrant Compote

4 ½ cups redcurrants, stalks removed

1 cup redcurrant juice

4 tbsp sugar

Bring the redcurrants to the boil with the juice and sugar and continue to cook for about 2 minutes.

Apple Compote

1 lb tart apples

juice of 1 lemon

½ cup water

½ cup sugar

1 cinnamon stick

Peel and core the apples, and cut into quarters.

Place in a saucepan, and add the lemon juice, water, sugar and cinnamon.

Place the lid on the pot, bring to the boil, then simmer over a low heat for about 10 minutes.

Discard the cinnamon stick before serving.

Deep-Fried Potatoes

You buy an order of golden french fries. They are still a bit too hot but you cannot wait to tuck in – it's an experience we have all shared. However, real gourmets fry their own. They can be sure the fat is really fresh, making the fries taste even better.

Deep-frying is quite easy. All you need is hot vegetable oil – and plenty of it! First heat it in a deep-fryer to at least 350°F. If you do not have a kitchen thermometer, you can test the oil with a wooden spoon. The fat is hot enough when little bubbles rise from the spoon. Then add the french fries, croquettes or potato balls (you will find the recipes on the following pages).

To avoid the fat cooling down too much, it is best to fry only a small batch of potatoes at a time. Take the potatoes out of the oil after a few minutes – as soon as the outsides are crisp and golden. Drain them briefly on paper towels, then serve piping hot.

119

French Fries

2 ¼ lb baking potatoes
oil for deep-frying
salt

Wash and peel the potatoes.

First slice the potatoes, then cut them into sticks.

Rinse, drain in a colander, and pat thoroughly dry with paper towels.

Heat the oil to 250°F, and blanch the potatoes in batches for 3 minutes each.

Remove the potatoes from the oil and drain on paper towels.

Meanwhile, reheat the oil to 350°F, then return the potatoes to the oil and fry until crisp and golden.

Drain on paper towels and serve sprinkled with salt.

You can also use frozen french fries, in which case follow the instructions on the package.

Serves 4
500 calories per serving

Pepper Steak

4 fillet mignon,
  each weighing 7 oz

3 tbsp oil

1 tbsp butter

salt

½ cup white wine

1 cup light cream

2 tbsp green peppercorns

freshly ground pepper

Heat the oil in a skillet and sear the steaks over a high heat.

Turn down the heat, add the butter and fry the steaks for 10–15 minutes, turning several times.

Remove the steaks from the skillet, season with salt on both sides, wrap in aluminum foil and keep warm.

Pour off the excess fat in the skillet. Pour the wine into the remaining juices.

Reduce the liquid by half, then add the cream and reduce by one-third.

Add the green peppercorns to the sauce and season to taste with salt and pepper. Pour the sauce over the steaks, and serve with French Fries.

Serves 4
525 calories per serving
Recommended salad: 3

Chicken in Mushroom Sauce

1 roasting chicken

salt

freshly ground pepper

2 tbsp oil

1 tbsp butter

1 onion, finely chopped

½ cup white wine

1 cup light cream

2 ½ cups button mushrooms

a little lemon juice

Divide the chicken into 8 pieces and season with salt and pepper.

Heat the oil and butter in a saucepan, and fry the chicken until brown all over.

Pour off the excess fat, then add the onion, and sauté.

Add the wine, bring to the boil, then reduce slightly.

Add the cream and gently simmer over a low heat for 30 minutes.

Clean and finely slice the mushrooms.

Add the mushrooms to the skillet 10 minutes before the end of the cooking time.

Season to taste with salt, pepper and lemon juice.

Serve with French Fries.

Serves 4
353 calories per serving

123

Croquette Potatoes

18 oz potatoes

2 egg yolks

salt

nutmeg

2 tbsp finely chopped parsley

flour for coating

1 beaten egg

breadcrumbs for coating

oil for deep-frying

Peel the potatoes and cook them in boiling salted water for about 20 minutes.

Drain in a colander, allow to cool a little, then, while still hot, mash until smooth.

Stir in the egg yolks, and season with salt and nutmeg.

Mix the chopped parsley into the potatoes, them shape into small, thick rolls.

Coat the croquettes first in flour, then in beaten egg and finally in breadcrumbs.

Fry in oil at 350°F for 5 minutes until golden.

Serves 4
350 calories per serving

Rabbit in Mustard Sauce

4 rabbit forelegs

salt

freshly ground pepper

2 tbsp oil

½ cup white wine

½ cup crème fraîche

3 tbsp coarse-grained mustard

1 bunch tarragon, finely chopped

1 bunch spring carrots

2 tbsp butter

1 ¾ cups canned chestnuts

½ cup honey

Season the rabbit with salt and pepper.

Heat the oil in a saucepan, and fry the rabbit until browned all over.

Roast in the oven at 400˚F for 20 minutes, then wrap in aluminum foil and leave to stand.

Pour off the excess fat from the roasting pan.

Add the wine to the remaining juices, then add the crème fraîche and simmer for 5 minutes.

Season with salt, pepper and mustard.

Add the tarragon, but do not return to the boil.

Scrape the carrots and cook in salted water until tender but still crisp.

Melt the butter and toss the carrots in it.

Heat the chestnuts through with the juice from the can and the honey.

Serve the rabbit with the sauce, carrots, chestnuts and Potato Croquettes.

Serves 4
574 calories per serving
Recommended salad: 2

Almond Potato Balls

2 ¼ lb potatoes

1 egg yolk

salt

flour for coating

1 beaten egg

breadcrumbs for coating

1 cup flaked almonds

oil for deep-frying

Wash and peel the potatoes, then cut them into chunks.

Boil in salted water for about 20 minutes, drain in a colander and allow to cool a little.

Mash the potatoes until smooth, stir in the egg yolk and season with salt.

Shape into small balls, and coat them first in flour, next in beaten egg, then in breadcrumbs and finally in almond flakes.

Fry in oil at about 325°F for about 4 minutes until golden brown.

Serves 4
306 calories per serving

Breast of Pheasant with Figs and Pepper Sauce

4 pheasant breasts
salt
freshly ground pepper
1 pig's caul (order from the butcher) or thin slices of unsmoked bacon
1 tbsp oil
1 tbsp butter
2 red bell peppers
1 cup light cream
8 oz canned figs in syrup

Season the pheasant breasts with salt and pepper.

Arrange each pair of breasts with the fleshy sides towards each other and wrap in half the caul and secure tightly. If you cannot obtain a caul, use very thin slices of unsmoked bacon.

Heat the oil and butter in an ovenproof casserole, and brown the pheasant breasts all over.

Roast in the oven at 400°F for 15–20 minutes, basting frequently with the pan juices.

Remove the meat from the oven, wrap in aluminum foil and keep warm.

Broil the peppers until blisters form on the skins. Remove from the broiler and peel while still hot.

Coarsely chop 1 ½ peppers, and cut the remaining half into diamond shapes.

Pour the cream into a saucepan, add the chopped peppers and bring to the boil, then simmer for 5 minutes.

Purée in a blender and season with salt and pepper.

Add the pepper diamonds to the sauce.

In another saucepan briefly warm the figs in their syrup.

Carve the pheasant breasts diagonally into slices.

Serve with the sauce, figs and Almond Potato Balls.

Serves 4
400 calories per serving

Venison in Gingerbread Sauce

2 tbsp oil

1 ¾ lb haunch of venison

salt

freshly ground pepper

1 cup red wine

1 cup game stock

3 slices gingerbread cake

1 tbsp cornstarch

7 tbsp butter, straight from the refrigerator, cut into small pieces

2 ½ cups oyster mushrooms

1 tbsp butter

1 bunch parsley, finely chopped

1 ½ cups preserved gooseberries

3 tbsp sugar

juice of 1 lemon

2 tbsp water

Heat the oil in a large, ovenproof casserole and brown the venison all over.

Season with salt and pepper, then roast in the oven at 400°F for 20 minutes.

Pour the wine over the meat and cook for a further 20–30 minutes, basting frequently.

Remove the meat from the oven, wrap in aluminum foil and keep warm.

Add the stock to the pan juices, crumble in the gingerbread, then reduce the sauce by half. Strain the sauce through a sieve, then bind with cornstarch.

Stir the chilled butter into the sauce.

Clean the oyster mushrooms, discarding the tough stalks.

Heat 1 tablespoon of butter in a skillet and sauté the mushrooms.

Season with salt and pepper, and sprinkle with parsley.

Place the gooseberries in a saucepan with sugar, lemon juice and water, and bring briefly to the boil.

Carve the venison into thin slices and arrange on individual plates.

Serve with sauce, oyster mushrooms, gooseberries and Potato Pears.

Potato Pears

2 ¼ lb potatoes

1 egg

flour for coating

1 beaten egg

breadcrumbs for coating

salt

freshly ground pepper

cloves

Wash and peel the potatoes and cut them into chunks.

Cook in salted water for about 20 minutes, then drain in a colander and leave to cool.

Mash the potatoes until smooth, stir in the egg, and season with salt and pepper.

With wet hands, form the mashed potatoes into small pear shapes.

Coat the potato pears first in flour, then in beaten egg and finally in breadcrumbs.

Deep-fry in oil at a temperature of 350°F for about 5 minutes until they are a light golden brown, then drain on paper towels.

Garnish each pear, using a clove as the "flower" and a parsley stem as the "stalk".

Serves 4
724 calories per serving

Deep-Fried Vegetables in Beer Batter

4 small beets

1 bunch small white turnips

1 bunch carrots

4 young leeks

9 oz potatoes

1 ¾ cups sifted flour

1 cup beer

1 tsp salt

4 egg whites, stiffly beaten

oil for deep-frying

Clean and peel the vegetables.

Cook the beets in boiling salted water for 20 minutes, then drain in a colander. Allow to cool completely before slicing.

Cut the leeks into diagonal pieces. Leave the turnips and carrots whole. Cook the turnips, carrots and leeks separately in boiling water, or steam, until tender but still crisp.

Drain in a colander and rinse under cold running water.

Peel the potatoes and boil in salted water for about 20 minutes. Drain in a colander and allow to cool a little, then mash until smooth.

Mix the flour, beer and salt. Add to the mashed potatoes and mix to a smooth batter.

Very carefully fold in the egg whites.

Coat the vegetables in the batter and deep-fry in oil at 350°F for 6–7 minutes.

Options

Try cooking other vegetables, such as broccoli, baby corncobs, celery and peppers, in the same way.

Serves 4

409 calories per serving

Potato Nests

2 ¼ lb baking potatoes

oil for deep-frying

salt

1 bunch young beets

1 bunch small white turnips

1 bunch spring carrots

6 tbsp butter

1 bunch parsley, finely chopped

1 bunch basil, cut into thin strips

Peel and thinly slice the potatoes, then cut them into matchsticks. Wash and drain in a sieve, and dry thoroughly with paper towels.

Using a double basket (see photo), deep-fry in batches in oil at 350°F for 6–7 minutes.

Drain on paper towels and sprinkle with salt.

Clean and peel the vegetables.

Cook the beets in boiling salted water for 20 minutes. Drain in a colander. Cut into quarters when cold.

Cook the turnips and carrots in boiling salted water until tender but still crisp. Drain in a colander and rinse under cold running water.

Heat one-third of the butter in a skillet for each vegetable, and toss the vegetables separately. Sprinkle the carrots with parsley, and the turnips with basil.

Serve the potato nests with the vegetables.

Serves 4
355 calories per serving

Gratins and Bakes

Gratin dauphinois *is one of the most aristocratic of all potato dishes. Sliced and baked in the oven, topped with cheese and served as a side dish, the recipe for potatoes "in the style of the heir to the throne" is one of the simplest in the world.*

There are endless varieties of potato bakes. They can be served as appetizers in tiny dishes or provide a complete meal, packed with filling ingredients. For all their gold-encrusted splendor, they are also practical. You can prepare them in advance, then pop them in the oven when you are ready and bring them straight to the table.

139

Zucchini and Potato Gratin

— Use quiche pan —

1 lb. ~~9 oz~~	*potatoes, boiled in their skins*
½ lb ~~9 oz~~	*zucchini*

5 tbsp butter = 1 T. + ¼ cup

2 garlic cloves — finely chopped

salt

freshly ground pepper

1 bunch tarragon, finely chopped or 2 T. dried

1 cup light cream

½ cup grated Swiss cheese

Peel and slice the potatoes while they are still warm.

Wash and slice the zucchini.

Grease a baking dish with about 1 tablespoon of butter, and arrange the potatoes and zucchini in alternating, overlapping layers. Place the remaining butter in the refrigerator until needed.

Crush the garlic in a garlic press.

Stir the garlic, salt, pepper and tarragon into the cream.

Pour the cream over the vegetables, sprinkle with grated cheese and top with flakes of chilled butter. Bake in the oven at 425°F for 20–25 minutes until light golden brown.

Serves 4
373 calories per serving

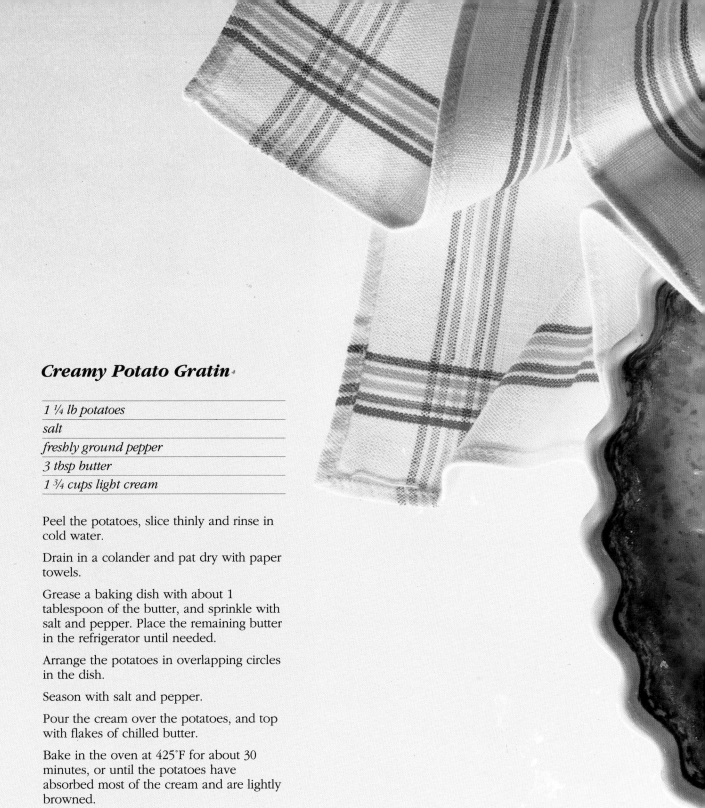

Creamy Potato Gratin

1 ¼ lb potatoes

salt

freshly ground pepper

3 tbsp butter

1 ¾ cups light cream

Peel the potatoes, slice thinly and rinse in cold water.

Drain in a colander and pat dry with paper towels.

Grease a baking dish with about 1 tablespoon of the butter, and sprinkle with salt and pepper. Place the remaining butter in the refrigerator until needed.

Arrange the potatoes in overlapping circles in the dish.

Season with salt and pepper.

Pour the cream over the potatoes, and top with flakes of chilled butter.

Bake in the oven at 425°F for about 30 minutes, or until the potatoes have absorbed most of the cream and are lightly browned.

Serves 4
434 calories per serving

Eggplant and Potato Bake

2 small eggplants (10 oz)

salt

4 tbsp olive oil

1 onion, finely chopped

1 garlic clove, finely chopped

14 oz tomatoes

1 bunch basil

1 ½ lb potatoes

7 oz mozzarella cheese

1 tbsp butter

freshly ground pepper

Slice the eggplants, sprinkle with salt and leave to stand with a weight on top for about 30 minutes. Pat dry with paper towels.

Heat 3 tablespoons of oil in a frying-pan and fry the eggplants, in batches if necessary, and set aside.

Heat the remaining oil in the skillet and sauté the onion and garlic.

Wash and coarsely chop the tomatoes. Add them to the garlic and onions, and simmer for 45 minutes.

Rub the tomatoes through a sieve and season with salt and pepper.

Cut the basil into thin strips and add to the sauce.

Peel and slice the potatoes.

Cook in boiling water for 5 minutes, then drain in a colander.

Drain and slice the mozzarella cheese.

Butter a baking dish, and arrange the eggplants, potatoes, mozzarella and tomato sauce in layers, finishing with tomato sauce and mozzarella.

Bake in the oven at 400°F for about 40 minutes.

Serves 4

313 calories per serving

Leek and Potato Gratin with Chervil

2 ¼ lb small new potatoes

14 oz leeks

salt

freshly ground pepper

4 tbsp butter

3 ½ cups chervil

1 ¾ cups light cream

Wash and scrub the potatoes.

Wash the leeks. Discard the dark green parts, then cut the remainder diagonally into pieces.

Cook the leeks in boiling salted water for 1 minute, drain in a colander and rinse under cold running water.

Grease a baking dish with about 1 tablespoon of the butter and line with the leeks. Place the remainder of the butter in the refrigerator until needed.

Arrange the potatoes on top of the leeks, and season with salt and pepper.

Sprinkle the chervil over the potatoes, then pour in the cream.

Sprinkle flakes of the chilled butter on top, then cover the dish with aluminum foil.

Bake in the oven at 400°F for about 60 minutes.

Serves 4
586 calories per serving

147

Mixed Vegetable Gratin

2 ¼ lb potatoes

3 ½ cups milk

1 cup butter

salt

freshly ground pepper

nutmeg

18 oz broccoli

1 bunch carrots

2–3 small kohlrabi

2 leeks

2 tbsp all-purpose flour

⅞ cup grated Swiss cheese

Peel the potatoes and cook in boiling salted water for about 20 minutes. Drain in a colander and allow to cool a little. Mash until smooth while still warm.

Bring 1 cup of the milk and 7 tablespoons of the butter to the boil together, then stir into the potatoes. Season with salt, pepper and nutmeg.

Wash and trim the vegetables, peeling if necessary. Divide the broccoli into flowerets. Slice the carrots and kohlrabi. Cut the leek into diagonal pieces.

Cook each vegetable separately in boiling salted water until tender but crisp, drain in a colander and rinse under cold water.

Heat 3 tablespoons of the butter, then stir in the flour. Slowly add the remaining milk, stirring constantly to avoid lumps forming. Bring to the boil, then simmer for 15 minutes.

Stir in the cheese and season the sauce with salt and pepper.

Grease a baking dish with 1 tablespoon butter, arrange the vegetables in layers in the dish, and pour over the cheese sauce. Chill the remaining butter until needed.

Put the potato purée in a pastry bag with a star-shaped tip and pipe on top of the vegetables.

Sprinkle with flakes of the chilled butter and bake in the oven at 350°F for 40 minutes.

Serves 4
937 calories per serving

Oven Specialties

Potatoes with Rosemary and Garlic

2 ¼ lb small baking potatoes

6 tbsp olive oil

6 cloves garlic

leaves from 3 sprigs rosemary

coarse salt

Wash, scrub and halve the potatoes. Arrange them in a roasting pan and drizzle with olive oil.

Peel the garlic and cut crosswise into thin slices.

Sprinkle the garlic and rosemary over the potatoes, and season with salt.

Cover the pan with waxed paper, and roast the potatoes in the oven at 400°F for about 20 minutes.

Remove from the oven, discard the waxed paper and turn the potatoes over.

Return to the oven for 25–30 minutes.

Serves 4
207 calories per serving
Recommended salad: 5

Baked Potatoes with Caviar

4 medium-sized baking potatoes

1 cup crème fraîche

salt

freshly ground pepper

1 bunch chives, finely chopped

3 tbsp caviar

Wash and scrub the potatoes. Wrap each potato in a piece of aluminum foil large enough to cover it completely.

Bake in the oven at 425°F for about 60 minutes.

Season the crème fraîche with salt and pepper, and stir in the chives.

Unwrap the potatoes and gently break open the tops with a fork.

Pile the crème fraîche on top, and serve sprinkled with caviar.

Serves 4
192 calories per serving

Potato Pie

18 oz potatoes

3 cups all-purpose flour

¾ cup butter

½ tsp salt

1 ¼ cups water

2 eggs

1 ½ cup finely diced Swiss cheese

2 egg yolks

½ cup milk

2 egg whites, stiffly beaten

Peel the potatoes and boil in salted water for about 20 minutes.

Drain in a colander and allow to cool a little.

Knead 2 ½ cups of the flour and 10 tablespoons of the butter together, add salt, one-third of the water and the 2 eggs, and work to a smooth dough.

On a floured pastry board, roll out the dough into a circular piece about 11 ½ inches in diameter.

Grease a suitably sized flan or tart dish with about 1 tablespoon of butter, and lay the pastry in the dish.

Mash the potatoes until smooth and stir in the cheese.

Mix the egg yolks with the remaining flour and water and the milk, then fold in the egg whites.

Carefully fold the egg mixture into the potatoes.

Fill the pastry shell with the potato and cheese mixture.

Bake in the oven at 400˚F for 30–40 minutes, until a light golden brown.

Serves 4
932 calories per serving

Apple Turnovers

2 ¼ lb potatoes

1 ¼ cups all-purpose flour

salt

2 eggs

7 tbsp clarified butter, melted

18 oz green apples

1 tbsp Calvados

¾ cup sugar

1 cup sour cream

flour for rolling

½ cup milk

1 tbsp ground cinnamon

Peel the potatoes and cook in boiling salted water for about 20 minutes.

Drain in a colander. Mash until smooth while still hot and leave to cool.

Add the flour, salt and eggs to the potatoes and knead to a dough. Shape the dough into a sausage, then cut into portions 2 ½ inches long.

On a floured surface, roll each portion into a circle about 6 inches in diameter, and brush with melted butter.

Peel and core the apples, then cut, first into quarters and then into thin slices. Sprinkle with Calvados. Leave to stand for 5 minutes, then arrange on top of the pastry circles, sprinkle with about ½ cup sugar and top each turnover with 1 tablespoon sour cream.

Roll up each turnover, folding the sides in and pressing the ends down firmly. Grease a baking dish with melted butter, arrange the turnovers tightly side by side, and brush with melted butter. Bake in the oven at 400°F for about 40 minutes.

When the top is lightly browned, heat the milk and pour over the turnovers.

Continue to cook until all the milk has been absorbed.

Mix the remaining sugar and cinnamon, and sprinkle over the turnovers.

Serves 4
831 calories per serving

Potato Soufflé

1 ⅔ lb potatoes

7 tbsp butter

3 egg yolks

1 cup freshly grated Swiss cheese

salt

nutmeg

3 egg whites, stiffly beaten

breadcrumbs for lining the dish

Peel the potatoes and cook them in salted water for about 20 minutes.

Drain in a colander and allow to cool a little.

Mash the potatoes until smooth and leave to cool a bit longer.

Stir about 4 tablespoons of the butter into the mashed potatoes a little at a time.

Add the egg yolks and just over half of the cheese, then season with salt and nutmeg.

Carefully fold in the egg whites.

Grease a soufflé dish with about 1 tablespoon of the butter, and line with breadcrumbs. Put the remaining butter into the refrigerator until needed.

Fill the dish three-quarters full with the potato mixture, sprinkle with the remaining cheese and top with flakes of chilled butter.

Bake in the oven at 400°F for about 60 minutes.

Serves 4
427 calories per serving

Bread and Cake

If you haven't tried it, you would never believe it: you can even make bread from potatoes. To amaze your friends, invite them to drop around for a snack and serve them the bread and rolls shown on the following pages. To enjoy them at their best, make sure you eat them fresh and still warm from the oven. Potatoes also make delicious cakes: try the recipe for Potato-Almond Cake.

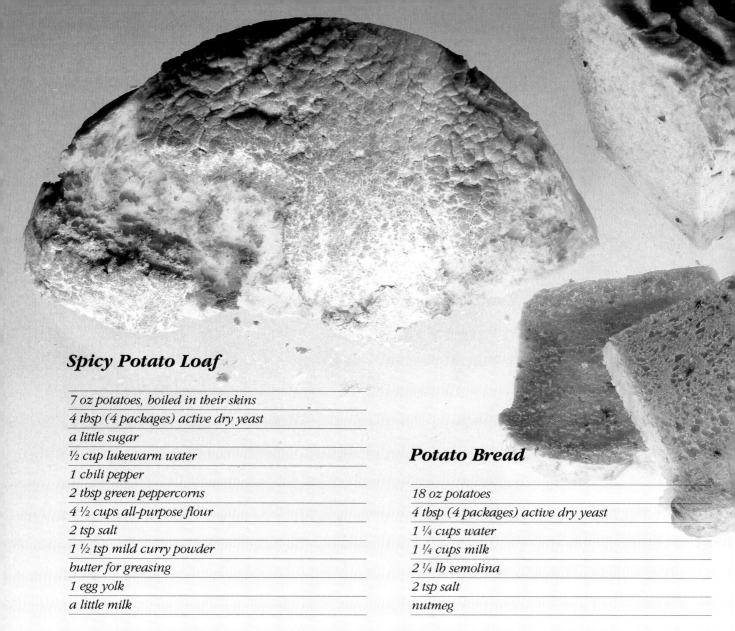

Spicy Potato Loaf

7 oz potatoes, boiled in their skins
4 tbsp (4 packages) active dry yeast
a little sugar
½ cup lukewarm water
1 chili pepper
2 tbsp green peppercorns
4 ½ cups all-purpose flour
2 tsp salt
1 ½ tsp mild curry powder
butter for greasing
1 egg yolk
a little milk

Peel the potatoes while still warm, and mash.

Dissolve the yeast and sugar in the lukewarm water.

Crush the chili pepper, using a pestle and mortar. Mix the mashed potatoes with the chili, green peppercorns, flour, salt and curry powder.

Add the yeast mixture to the flour and knead to a smooth dough, adding more water, as necessary. Cover the dough and leave to prove in a warm place for about 30 minutes. Knead thoroughly again.

Butter a loaf pan and place the dough in it.

Mix the egg yolk with milk, and use to brush the loaf. Score the top of the loaf in a diagonal pattern, then leave to prove for another 20 minutes.

Bake in the oven at 400°F for about 40 minutes.

Remove from the oven and allow to cool in the pan before turning out.

Potato Bread

18 oz potatoes
4 tbsp (4 packages) active dry yeast
1 ¼ cups water
1 ¼ cups milk
2 ¼ lb semolina
2 tsp salt
nutmeg

Peel the potatoes and boil them in salted water for about 20 minutes. Drain in a colander and leave to cool a little, then mash until smooth.

Dissolve the yeast in 6 tablespoons of mixed lukewarm water and milk.

Sift the semolina and salt into a bowl, add the nutmeg, then knead the potatoes with the semolina to make a smooth dough. Add the dissolved yeast and the remaining liquid to the dough and knead thoroughly.

Cover the dough and leave to prove in a warm place for about 2 hours, until it has doubled in volume.

Knead again thoroughly and, with floured hands, shape the dough into a round loaf. Stand the loaf on a floured baking sheet, cover with a damp cloth and leave to prove for a further 30 minutes.

Bake in the oven at 425°F for about 45 minutes, until crusty and golden brown.

162

Potato Brioche

1⅔ lb potatoes

2 eggs

2 tsp salt

cayenne pepper

nutmeg

butter for greasing

1 finger-thick slice Swiss cheese

4 tbsp butter, melted

breadcrumbs

Peel the potatoes and boil in salted water for about 20 minutes. Drain, then mash until smooth.

Place in the oven at minimum setting for about 12 minutes to dry out. Stir the eggs into the mashed potatoes to make a dough, and season with salt, cayenne pepper and nutmeg.

Divide the dough into two-thirds and one-third of the quantity. Shape the larger quantity into 10 balls to fit in a ramekin dish, and the smaller quantity into 10 smaller balls.

Butter 10 ramekins and place one large ball in each. Using a knife, make a groove about ½ inch deep across each ball.

Cut the cheese into 10 equal-sized cubes and insert 1 cube into each groove. Place a small ball on top of each brioche and brush with melted butter. Sprinkle with breadcrumbs and bake in the oven at 400°F for 15–20 minutes until the brioches are golden brown and crusty

Potato Sticks

5 oz potatoes

10 tbsp butter

1 ¼ cups all-purpose flour

salt

1 egg yolk

2 tbsp light cream

coarse salt

poppy seeds

caraway seeds

Peel the potatoes and boil in salted water for about 20 minutes. Drain in a colander and allow to cool.

Coarsely grate the potatoes. Mix the grated potatoes with butter and flour, and season with salt.

Knead to a smooth dough, divide into 4 portions and shape each portion into a roll. Cut each roll into 16 pieces.

Roll each piece into a "finger" and, using a knife, make several incisions across each one.

Beat the egg and cream together, and brush each finger with the mixture.

Sprinkle one-third of the sticks with salt, one-third with poppy seeds and the rest with caraway seeds. Bake in the oven at 400°F for 10–12 minutes until golden.

Potato Croissants

18 oz potatoes

salt

freshly ground pepper

20 black olives, stoned

1 tbsp oil

1 onion, finely chopped

¾ cup crumbled ewe's milk cheese

1 bunch parsley, finely chopped

frozen puff pastry

flour for rolling

1 egg yolk

2 tbsp light cream

1 tbsp coarse salt

Peel the potatoes and boil for about 20 minutes in salted water.

Drain in a colander, leave to cool a little, then mash until smooth and season with salt and pepper.

Coarsely chop the olives.

Heat the oil in a small skillet and sauté the onion.

Stir the olives, cheese, onions and parsley into the potatoes.

On a floured work surface, roll out the pastry dough and cut into rectangles 7 x 4 inches. Cut each piece into 2 triangles.

Place 1 tablespoon of filling on each triangle, then roll from the base to the point.

Beat the egg and cream together. Brush the croissants with the mixture, then sprinkle with salt.

Bake in the oven at 400°F for 15–20 minutes until golden.

Serves 4
507 calories per serving

Potato Strudel

2 ½ cups sifted all-purpose flour

1 egg

1 tsp salt

1 tsp oil

3 ½ fl oz warm water

½ tbsp vinegar

9 oz potatoes

6 tbsp butter

3 tbsp sugar

2 egg yolks

juice and grated peel of 1 lemon

½ cup finely ground almonds

½ cup light cream

⅓ cup sultanas or ½ cup raisins

2 egg whites, stiffly beaten

breadcrumbs

confectioner's sugar for dusting

Make a well in the middle of the sifted flour and add the egg, salt and oil. Mix the water and vinegar and add a little at a time to the flour, then quickly knead to a smooth dough. Leave to stand for about 15 minutes.

Peel the potatoes and boil them in salted water for about 20 minutes. Drain and mash until smooth while still hot.

Beat 4 tablespoons of butter until it becomes fluffy, and gradually stir in the sugar. Add the egg yolks and stir until creamy. Stir in the lemon peel and juice, almonds, cream and sultanas or raisins, then add to the dough and mix thoroughly. Fold in the egg whites.

Roll out the dough on a large floured cloth, then pull it into a thin sheet 20 x 28 inches. Sprinkle on the breadcrumbs, leaving a border of 1 ⅛ inch all around, and spread the filling on top. Starting at one of the long sides, roll the pastry up and firmly seal the edges.

Grease a baking sheet with about 1 tablespoon of butter and place the strudel on it. Melt the remaining butter and brush it over the strudel. Bake in the oven at 425°F for about 50 minutes until golden brown. Dust with confectioner's sugar.

Serves 4
777 calories per serving

Almond Cake

14 oz potatoes, boiled in their skins

⅞ cup sugar

8 eggs, separated

¾ cup finely chopped almonds

1 cup ground almonds

pinch each of salt, ground cloves and
  ground cardamom

grated peel of 1 lemon

pulp from ½ vanilla pod

butter for greasing

breadcrumbs to line the mold

½ lb (1 ⅓ cups) semi-sweet chocolate

Optional: confectioner's sugar for dusting

Cook the potatoes a day in advance. When you are ready to bake, peel and grate them.

Whisk the sugar and egg yolks until frothy, then fold in the grated potatoes.

Add the chopped and ground almonds, salt and spices, lemon peel and vanilla pulp, and stir thoroughly.

Beat the egg whites until stiff, then carefully fold into the mixture.

Grease a fluted cake mold about 10 inches in diameter with butter and sprinkle with breadcrumbs.

Pour the dough into the mold and bake in the oven at 400°F for about 60 minutes. **Do not** open the oven door during the baking time.

Turn off the heat and leave the cake to stand in the oven for a further 20 minutes.

Remove the cake from the oven and turn out onto a wire cooling rack.

Melt the chocolate and pour over the cake.

If you like, sprinkle with confectioner's sugar.

The cake will be very dark in color, but this does not spoil the flavor.

Serves 4
879 calories per serving

168

Side Salads

You don't have to be an artist to turn a salad into a work of art. Nature has designed salad leaves, vegetables and herbs in such a way that they create their own beautiful designs, so we urge you to serve salads on a flat plate rather than in a bowl. This also has advantages both for flavor and fragrance. Sprinkled sparingly over the salad, dressings combine with the ingredients without swamping them.

You can, of course, serve a salad with any potato dish. With many recipes in this book, we have suggested the salads that harmonize best with specific dishes.

1
Arugula with Quail Eggs

1 ½ cups arugula

8 quail eggs

¼ lb sliced smoked bacon

4 slices white bread, crusts removed

2 tbsp oil

1 small container cress

3 tbsp red wine vinegar

9 tbsp olive oil

salt

freshly ground pepper

Sort the arugula. Wash and drain thoroughly.

Place the quail eggs in boiling water and cook for 4 minutes, rinse under cold running water, then shell and halve.

Fry or broil the bacon until crisp.

Finely dice the bread. Heat the oil in a skillet and fry the bread until golden brown.

Chop the cress with kitchen shears.

For the dressing, combine the vinegar, olive oil, salt and pepper.

Toss the arugula in the dressing and arrange on individual plates. Arrange the quail eggs, bacon and croûtons on top, sprinkle with cress, and drizzle the rest of the dressing on top.

2
French Bean and Pear Salads

1 lb french beans

1 tbsp butter

7 tbsp pine-nuts

2 pears

20 red grapes

leaves of 1 bunch mint

3 tbsp cider vinegar

9 tbsp pistachio oil

salt

freshly ground pepper

Cut the ends off the beans, then cut diagonally into pieces. Place in boiling salted water and cook for 4 minutes. Drain in a colander and rinse under cold running water.

Heat the butter in a skillet and fry the pine-nuts until golden.

Thinly slice the pears and grapes lengthwise. Cut half the mint into thin strips.

To make the dressing, mix vinegar, oil, salt and pepper, and stir in the strips of mint.

Arrange the beans, pears and grapes on individual plates, and sprinkle with pine-nuts. Drizzle the dressing over the salad, and garnish with whole mint leaves.

3
Oak-Leaf Lettuce with Diced Vegetables

1 oak-leaf lettuce	
2 carrots, diced	
1 leek, light green parts only, diced	
½ stick celery, diced	
1 tomato, peeled, deseeded and diced	
7 tbsp oil	
1 onion, finely chopped	
1 cup mung-bean sprouts	
1 tbsp mustard	
3 tbsp red wine vinegar	
salt	
freshly ground pepper	
sugar	

Sort, wash and thoroughly dry the lettuce.

Cook the carrots, leek and celery in boiling water, or steam, until tender but still crisp. Drain in a colander, then rinse under cold running water.

Heat 1 tablespoon of oil in a skillet and sauté the onion until transparent.

Mix the onion with mustard, vinegar, the remaining oil, salt, pepper and sugar, then beat in a blender until frothy.

Toss the lettuce in the dressing and arrange on individual plates. Sprinkle with vegetables and bean sprouts, and drizzle the remaining dressing on top.

4
Grapefruit, Pomegranate and Radish Salad

1 green lettuce
1 lollo rosso
1 curly endive
1 small radicchio
1 pink grapefruit
1 pomegranate
1 bunch radishes
leaves from small bunch parsley
3 tbsp vinegar
9 tbsp oil
salt
freshly ground pepper
sugar

Sort, wash and thoroughly dry the salad leaves.

Peel the grapefruit, remove the pith and cut into wedges.

Remove the seeds from the pomegranate.

Slice the radishes.

Mix the vinegar, oil, salt, pepper and sugar for the dressing.

Toss the salad leaves in the dressing and arrange on individual plates.

Arrange the grapefruit, pomegranate seeds, radishes and parsley on top, then sprinkle with the rest of the dressing.

5
Tomato Salad

4 beefsteak tomatoes
2 shallots
1 bunch basil
3 tbsp balsamic vinegar
9 tbsp olive oil
salt
freshly ground pepper

Wash the tomatoes, remove the stalks and the hard flesh surrounding them, then slice lengthwise.

Peel the shallots and cut crosswise into thin slices.

Tear off the basil leaves.

To make the dressing, mix the vinegar, oil, salt and pepper.

Arrange the tomatoes and shallots on individual plates, and drizzle the dressing on top. Serve sprinkled with basil.

6
Endive and
Beet Salad

4 endive bulbs

2 beets

1 bunch chives

3 tbsp lemon juice

9 tbsp peanut oil

½ cup capers

salt

freshly ground pepper

Separate the endive, discarding the bitter stalk. Wash and leave to drain.

Cook the beets in boiling salted water for 20 minutes. Drain in a colander and leave to cool.

Peel the beets and cut into thin strips.

Wash the chives and cut diagonally into long strips.

To make the dressing, mix the lemon juice, oil, salt and pepper, then stir in the capers.

Arrange the endive and beets on individual plates and drizzle the dressing on top. Serve sprinkled with chives.

7
Green Asparagus and Walnut Salad

2 ¼ lb green asparagus, woody ends removed
1 cup shelled walnuts, chopped
1 bunch watercress
3 tbsp raspberry vinegar
9 tbsp walnut oil
salt
freshly ground pepper

Cook the asparagus in boiling salted water, or steam, until tender but still crisp. Drain in a colander, briefly rinse under cold water, then drain again.

Wash the watercress and tear off the leaves. Cut half the leaves into thin strips.

To make the dressing, mix the vinegar, oil, salt and pepper, then stir in the chopped watercress.

Arrange the asparagus and walnuts on individual plates, and drizzle the dressing on top. Serve sprinkled with watercress leaves.

8
Avocado Salad with Caviar Cream Dressing

2 ripe avocados

lemon juice

10 cherry tomatoes

1 bunch tarragon

1 cup crème fraîche

¼ cup light cream

3 tbsp (2 oz) salmon caviar

salt

freshly ground pepper

Peel and halve the avocados, removing the stones. Slice the avocados crosswise, and sprinkle with lemon juice. Slice the cherry tomatoes crosswise.

Finely chop 1–2 stalks of tarragon. Tear off the leaves from the rest of the bunch.

To make the dressing, mix the crème fraîche, cream, salt, pepper and chopped tarragon.

Pour the dressing onto individual plates. Arrange the avocados and tomatoes on top, and serve sprinkled with caviar and tarragon leaves.

Vinegar and Oil

It is the dressing that turns a few green leaves into an exquisite salad. And it is vinegar and oil that make the dressing. There is such a wide range of both that you could create a new and exciting dressing every day. Vinegar and oil should be combined to make the best of their individual flavors. Pungent vinegars, like raspberry and sherry, should be used with subtly flavored oil. Similarly, strong-tasting oils, such as hazelnut or walnut, combine best with neutral-flavored vinegar. Some of the vinegars and oils described on the following pages are widely available; others might be found in delicatessens and speciality food stores.

Potato vinegar

Vinegar essence

Fruit vinegar Herb vinegar

Balsamic vinegar

Sherry vinegar

Raspberry vinegar

Vinegar brings out the flavor of herbs and spices, but only when used sparingly so that the acidity is not overwhelming. Since some varieties are more acidic than others, getting the right mix is a matter of trial and error. Vinegar makes raw food more digestible because it stimulates the digestive juices, so vinegar is healthy too.

Pumpkin-seed oil

Hazelnut oil

Sesame oil

Walnut oil

Grapeseed oil

Olive oil

Pistachio oil

Oil makes salad leaves smoother and helps the dressing to cling to them. If you really enjoy the taste of oil, always choose the cold-pressed sort. Hot-pressed oils, or those extracted by chemical means and refined, lose their distinctive flavour and, unfortunately, some of their health-giving properties.

183

Glossary

Balsamic vinegar
Dark brown, mild, sweet and fragrant – for many people, this is the finest of all vinegars. An Italian specialty, it is made from grape must. The longer it is left to mature, the thicker it becomes. The most famous balsamic vinegars, some up to 20 years old, come from Modena. Some of them are even sold as "vintage" vinegars.

Champagne vinegar
Produced from champagne, the aroma of this vinegar is more delicate than that of white-wine vinegar, but the flavor is similar.

Cider vinegar
Mild and fruity, this familiar vinegar is produced from apple must or from ripe apples.

Herb vinegars
These vinegars are based on wine or spirit vinegar, to which various kinds of aromatic herbs are added. The best kinds are made from pure wine vinegar with a single fresh herb, not herb extract.

Potato vinegar
Mildly acid, with a subtle potato flavor, this German speciality is made from potato spirit to which newly pressed potato juice has been added.

Raspberry vinegar
Wine vinegar matured with fresh raspberries has a delicate raspberry smell and flavor.

Sherry vinegar
Resembling sherry both in smell and subtle flavor, this vinegar is made from a blend of wine and sherry.

Wine vinegar
The best kinds of wine vinegar have a strong wine flavor. In some of them you can even detect the grape variety. The color depends on whether red or white wine has been used.

Grapeseed oil
This is a dark green oil, extracted from dried seeds of wine grapes, and has an almost neutral taste. Since it contains a high proportion of unsaturated fatty acids, it is regarded as particularly healthy.

Hazelnut oil
Cold-pressed from hazelnuts, this oil has a strong, very nutty flavor. It turns rancid after only a few months, so should be bought only in small quantities.

Herb oil

The flavor varies according to which herbs have been added: tarragon, basil, rosemary, thyme or a mixture of Provençal herbs. It also depends on the quality of the oil. Cold-pressed, neutral-tasting oil is used to produce the best herb oils.

Linseed oil

Produced from the seed of the flax plant, also known as linseed, this oil has a strong and very distinctive nutty flavor, but does not keep for long.

Olive oil

Olives can vary in flavor from very mild to powerful. The colors range from pale yellow to dark green, but this is no indicator of quality. The best olive oil, called "first pressing" and usually labelled as "extra virgin olive oil" is cold-pressed from fresh olives. Italy, Spain, France and Greece all produce cold-pressed oil, but the finest of all comes from the oil mills of Tuscany and Liguria.

Peanut oil

If it is cold-pressed, the oil has a strong peanut flavor. Usually, however, it is extracted and refined, and the flavor is somewhat neutral with only a hint of peanuts.

Pumpkin-seed oil

This oil has an intense, exquisitely nutty flavor and is very dark green in color (the darker the color, the better the quality). It is cold-pressed from the seeds of a special kind of pumpkin and is not widely available.

Salad and cooking oil

Pale vegetable oils with a completely neutral taste are hot-pressed or extracted from a variety of oils, including peanut, corn, sunflower and soya oils. To give them better keeping qualities, they are chemically purified (refined). They are not recommended for salads.

Sesame oil

The sesame seeds are roasted before being cold-pressed. The oil has a pleasant, nutty taste. Dark sesame oil has a stronger flavor than the lighter sort.

Walnut oil

With its mild and distinctly nutty taste, this is an aristocrat among oils, especially suited for refined salads. Once opened, it will keep for only a few months.

A large proportion of the potatoes we eat are processed. For people who shop only occasionally or have limited time in which to prepare meals, products such as canned peeled potatoes, potato salad and instant mashed potato are invaluable.

There is, of course, also a vast range of potato snacks. In addition to potato hoops, twirls and sticks, there is the chip, which is made in a seemingly endless variety of flavors and shapes.

Processed Potato Products

Frozen
Potato
Products

The new generation of potato products come to us ready-made, straight from the freezer and can be cooked in the oven in a matter of minutes. They take even less time in the microwave. No wonder sales of frozen french fries, croquettes, waffles and hash browns are on the increase. Even people concerned about following a healthy diet can enjoy them with a clear conscience. The quick-freezing procedures used by the food industry retain most of the potato's vital nutrients.

Index of Recipes